CELEBRATING THE LEGACY OF

BRETT FAVRE

AMERICA'S QUARTERBACK

Photography by Vernon Biever except where noted otherwise.
Content packaged by Mojo Media, Inc.
Editor: Joe Funk
Creative Director: Jason Hinman

This book is available in quantity at special discounts for your group or organization.
For further information, contact:

Triumph Books
542 South Dearborn Street
Suite 750
Chicago, IL 60605
Phone: (312) 939-3330
Fax: (312) 663-3557

Printed in the United States of America
ISBN: 978-1-60078-110-0

Getty Images

CONTENTS

AP/Wide World

Fun and Games

The rain began to fall an hour before kickoff.

It was a typical Florida downpour that came out of nowhere and cut through the humid Tampa air. But while the downpour sent fans at Houlihan's Stadium running for cover, Green Bay Packers quarterback Brett Favre walked out of the locker room and into the rain. That's when he smiled.

He looked up into the rain, opened his mouth, and let the water pelt him as if he were a six-year-old pounding through puddles in his backyard.

This was Brett Favre's element. This was where he belonged. This was football the way it was meant to be played all those years ago when the game was still a game.

The rain was his official cleansing from an off-season that could not have gone much worse. He stood in the rain and let it wash over him.

He was clean. He was fresh. He was ready to start over.

It was time.

It was September 1, 1996, and Favre was already an NFL star who was building his status as a Packers icon and, perhaps one day, a legitimate Hall of Famer.

But despite an NFL MVP award from the previ-ous season, the questions were already being asked about the young, talented, reckless quarterback of a team on the rise.

Could he deliver when it mattered most? Could he make the smart plays? Could he direct his team into places it had never been before?

He had a great arm and great skills, but did he have that indefinable something that would make him stand out from other quarterbacks?

And, most important on this sultry day in September, could he leave the past behind?

Little more than three months earlier, Brett Favre was stuck in a drug rehabilitation center in Kansas, and his future was not his own. Years of pounding and injury had sent Favre over the edge, and he found himself addicted to the painkiller Vicodin. Add to that his love of alcohol, and Favre was in trouble.

The stories were already legendary in Green Bay about Favre's late-night carousing, his infamous golf adventures that included a lot more than 7 irons, and, amazingly, his ability to shake it all off when it was time to play.

But what no one really knew, and what Favre always did his best to ignore, were the injuries.

(opposite) By 1996 Brett Favre was already an NFL star who was building his status as a Packers icon.

There were so many injuries—from nagging bumps to the kind that would have sent most players to the sideline. From a bad shoulder to damaged ankles. From rib injuries to banged-up toes, and, seemingly, everything in between. He never missed game; he never backed away; he never showed any signs of weakness. He couldn't.

And that hubris cost him.

So, for at least two years, Favre fell under the seductive influence of Vicodin, a powerful prescription painkiller.

He took it as recommended initially, to alleviate the nagging, gnawing pain that would overwhelm him on occasion. Then, as the pain increased and lingered, he found himself taking more of the drug. Then a little more and then a little more.

Soon, he was sometimes taking six tablets at a time and, finally, he was in the clutches of a full-blown addiction.

And this was all occurring as Favre was building his reputation as one of the rising, great young quarterbacks in the NFL.

He had taken over the Packers in 1992, an unknown reject from the Atlanta Falcons for whom the Packers, incredibly, had given away a first-round draft pick to obtain in a trade.

He was rough and raw and untamed. He would play the game the only way he knew how—with his hair on fire and from the seat of his pants. His throwing mechanics were terrible and his decisions sometimes left even the most casual football fan slack-jawed.

But he was proving he was a winner, and his teammates would run through a wall for him. And every year, the Packers got a little bit better.

In 1995, he led the Packers to their first NFC Championship Game in 20 years. And although they were beaten by the better and more experienced Dallas Cowboys, Favre had thrown 38 touchdown passes that season and was named the NFL's Most Valuable Player.

The future, it seemed, could not have been brighter as the Packers pointed to the 1996 season.

Which is why Packers fans, and the NFL in general, stood back in amazement when Favre announced in May 1996 that he was going into rehab to kick an addiction to prescription medication and alcohol. It was an announcement straight out of nowhere, a thunderbolt that stunned all but his girlfriend, Deanna, and his family.

It was the end of Brett Favre, many believed. At age 27, he was through, tripped up by his own arrogance and belief that nothing could harm him. What a waste. What a shame.

Favre descended into 45 days of rehab in Topeka, Kansas, and the biggest question was, what kind of a player—and more important, what kind of a person—would he be when he emerged?

In what amounted to perfect irony, when Favre finally left Topeka, it was just about time for Packers training camp to begin. In a carefully orchestrated, and packed, press conference in which coach Mike Holmgren sat by his star quarterback's side, Favre admitted his shortcomings.

He told of his struggles and his problems, but thanks to Holmgren's insistence that Favre say as much as possible without really saying anything at all, Favre said he was ready to move forward.

He read, again, a carefully prepared statement in which he admitted the next few days, weeks,

(opposite) Favre had taken over the Packers in 1992, an unknown reject from the Atlanta Falcons for whom the Packers, incredibly, gave away a first-round draft pick to obtain in a trade.

months, and years were not going to be easy.

But, he added, "I will not be defeated by this challenge."

Two months later, on a rainy afternoon in Tampa, Florida, he was ready to face that challenge. No one knew what would happen to Favre when he was hurt again. What could he take for the pain that was sure to emerge? No one knew if his heart was still in football. No one knew if he even had the skills anymore.

But Favre knew.

All through training camp, when he would talk about his off-season (which wasn't often), he always said the same thing.

"Go ahead. Bet against me."

That became his rallying cry, his mantra.

Don't think I can do it? Go ahead. Bet against me.

And against a young Tampa Bay Buccaneers squad that itself was ready to make its way onto the national stage under new coach Tony Dungy, Brett Favre answered his legion of doubters.

Favre completed 20 of 27 passes for 247 yards and four touchdowns as the Packers routed the Bucs 34–3.

(opposite) In 1995, Favre led the Packers to their first division title in 13 years and to the NFC Championship game, where they were beaten by the better and more experienced Dallas Cowboys. (above) When Favre is having fun, it's a sight to behold.

He looked smooth, calm, confident. He looked like the Brett Favre who had stepped off the field at the end of the 1995 season. He had met perhaps the biggest roadblock of his life and stepped seamlessly over it. He looked like he was having fun, and when Brett Favre is having fun, it's a sight to behold.

"I told you," he said to the gathered national media afterward. "Bet against me. Bet against me and you'll lose."

That is Brett Favre in a nutshell. Or in as much of a nutshell as you can fit him.

He was never like anyone else who had played the quarterback position from the time he was a kid and was coached by his beloved dad, Irvin. He was the same guy as a rookie with the Atlanta Falcons when he locked horns with a guy just as stubborn as he was—coach Jerry Glanville.

He never changed (well, he changed a little) when he came to Green Bay and adapted, as best he could, to the strictures placed on him by another man just as stubborn as he was—coach Mike Holmgren.

But that pairing proved magical. Holmgren wanted a young, strong-armed quarterback to run

(opposite) Mike Holmgren wanted a young, strong-armed quarterback to run his offense, and Favre wanted a chance to prove he belonged. (above) Favre has dealt with injuries, criticism, uncertainty, and even doubt as he began to wonder if he had worn out his welcome.

his offense, and Favre wanted a chance to prove he belonged. The two of them thundered back and forth. They fought, they made up, they fought again, and eventually, they began to understand that each knew what the other was doing.

Holmgren would talk to Favre as if he were his misbehaving son, and Favre would roll his eyes and take his coach's advice like a teenager waiting impatiently for the keys to the car.

There are a thousand Favre-Holmgren stories—but only a fraction of them can be told in public.

For example, in the middle of the Packers' 1996 NFC Championship Game against the Carolina Panthers in brutal sub-zero weather at Lambeau Field, Holmgren, his red face twisted in angst, called Favre to the sideline.

Holmgren was telling his quarterback what play he wanted him to run when he saw Favre looking at him and smiling.

"What the hell's so funny?" Holmgren asked.

"Your snot has frozen to your mustache," Favre said simply.

Two plays later, Favre fired a touchdown pass to Antonio Freeman to give Green Bay the lead and send the Packers to the Super Bowl.

It was, and really still is, a relationship neither man will ever have again and one neither will ever forget.

That was never made so clear than in one of the most poignant moments in Favre's career.

It was September 12, 1999, the first game of the season and the first game of Favre's career without Holmgren on the sideline. His coach was gone, having departed a few months earlier for the Seattle Seahawks, who paid him $7 million a season to become head coach and general manager, a title Holmgren had always coveted.

In his place came Ray Rhodes, the humorless anti-Holmgren who had once compared losing to having someone break into his home to rape and murder his family.

It was a tough training camp for Favre, who had to deal with recurring elbow soreness in his throwing arm and learn about life without Holmgren. There was also the nagging realization that, maybe, the Packers were on the downward slide after four years of uninterrupted success.

In that season opener against the Oakland Raiders, Favre struggled, throwing three interceptions and completing barely 50 percent of his passes. But as badly as the Packers played, Favre led them on two final, frantic, fourth-quarter drives that ended with touchdown passes to Corey Bradford and, as the game-winner in the final seconds, to tight end Jeff Thomason.

In the media interview room afterward, a visibly shaken and weary Favre stopped to compose himself. But he never did.

He looked down and the tears came. He said simply, "Sorry guys" and left the podium.

It was another roadblock, and he stepped over that one, too. Indeed, it seems there has always been something standing in Brett Favre's way.

He is football's version of Job, handling everything that comes his way and, somehow, growing stronger for all of it.

He dealt with a car crash that nearly killed him in college. Two weeks later, after having three feet of his intestine removed, he engineered his Southern Mississippi team to a stunning upset of Alabama.

He, of course, dealt with his alcohol and drug

(opposite) Convinced of his own ability, certain that he was doing what he always knew to be right, handling things in his own way, Favre has succeeded despite an ever-changing cast of teammates.

addiction. He shaved his head in sympathy for his wife Deanna, who was diagnosed with breast cancer in 2004.

The previous season, his dad had died of a heart attack in Mississippi the day before the Packers had a crucial Monday night game against the Oakland Raiders. He proceeded to play a game for the ages—completing 22 of 30 passes for 399 yards and four touchdowns. That game even left the normally nasty Raiders fans weeping in support.

He has seen his brother-in-law die in an ATV accident. He has dealt with a brother and a sister who were caught in legal issues. He watched his beloved Mississippi bayou destroyed by Hurricane Katrina. He huddled with his youngest daughter, Breleigh, in the basement of his home as a tornado roared overhead.

He has dealt with injuries, criticism, uncertainty, and, yes, even doubt as he began to wonder if even he had stayed too long at the party.

And he has done it all in public. Whether he really wanted to or not wasn't the issue. By the very nature of who he was and what he did, Favre's anguish was out there for all to see. And the more people who knew, it seemed, the better he performed.

He has watched dozens of teammates come and go. His best friends—like fellow quarterbacks Mark Brunell, Ty Detmer, and Doug Pederson, center Frank Winters, safety LeRoy Butler, tight end Mark Chmura—either retired, were cut, or were traded.

Others, like the inimitable defensive end Reggie White and enigmatic linebacker Wayne Simmons, died.

Coaches have come and gone, and faces have rolled by that Favre never knew before they were already gone.

But it's 2007 and Favre has survived it all.

Convinced of his own ability, certain that he was doing what he always knew to be right, handling things in his own way, Favre is enjoying a renaissance of a sort.

Now fronting the youngest team in the NFL and playing with guys who used to have his poster on their walls when they were kids, Favre has the Packers competitive again. And, here's the thing, the 38-year-old fogey has seemingly never had as much fun as he is now.

And on September 30, playing in the Metrodome, a site of far too many Favre nightmares over the years, he zipped a 16-yard touchdown pass to Greg Jennings. That score was the 421st of his career and set the NFL record for most touchdown passes in a career.

The old mark, held by Miami's Dan Marino, appeared for years to be one of those marks that might never be broken. And while Favre swore the win over the Vikings meant more than the record, it was clear that that record, among the dozens he owns, was special.

Favre's career has never been about the records. He has said that for years, and oddly, it's easy to believe.

He holds nearly every meaningful NFL throwing record, including touchdown passes, attempts, completions, victories, and, yes, interceptions. He will eventually take Marino's record for career passing yardage, and of course, his mark for most games started may never be touched.

It has not always been easy and there has been

(opposite) Ron Wolf saw Favre as a franchise-altering quarterback when few others did.

plenty of controversy—much due to Favre himself.

After all, there was a reason the Atlanta Falcons gave up the young hotshot after only one season. He practiced poorly. His attitude was awful. His late-night antics enraged Glanville and the front office. He was the worst kind of player: a cocksure kid convinced of his own greatness who had done absolutely nothing to prove it.

That's why the Falcons were so anxious to part with him after one season when Packers general manager Ron Wolf offered a first-round draft pick.

Of course, in subsequent years, the Falcons were ridiculed for giving up so quickly on a quarterback who ended up doing what Favre has done.

"I don't blame them for trading me," Favre said. "I would have traded me, too."

But hindsight is perfect, and no one, not even the Packers, could have predicted what would happen in Green Bay.

And it's easy to forget that, after the initial blush of success in Green Bay, Favre was horrible in 1993, throwing 24 interceptions and coming closer than most people realize to losing his starting job.

Holmgren had grown impatient with his young star and the stupid, pointless mistakes he made. It was only an intercession by then quarterbacks coach Steve Mariucci, and a close Favre friend even today, that saved the day.

He appealed to Holmgren for more patience and he told Favre to pull himself together and become the player everyone thought he could be.

Favre has opened his mouth too often for his own good. He has scolded players like Sterling Sharpe and Javon Walker for letting contract disputes get in the way of the team. He damaged his reputation in 2001 when, in the last game of the season, he fell down in front of his good buddy, New York Giants defensive end Michael Strahan, giving Strahan the NFL single-season sack record.

Favre denied he did anything on purpose, but teammates were furious because they knew the truth.

"That's not the Brett I know," tackle Mark Tauscher said.

And prior to the 2006 season, Favre kept the fans, the NFL, and, worst of all, his teammates and front office in limbo as he tried to decide whether he wanted to play another season.

It became an embarrassment and a distraction as new coach Mike McCarthy tried to assemble a plan while waiting on the most important player he had.

Eventually, of course, Favre decided to return and he had more fun than probably even he expected to have. The Packers were a young, frisky team that learned to win and had a ball doing it. As a result, Favre felt the years melt away.

Now he is the elder statesman, the lion in winter, the guy everyone looks to. And, amazingly, he continues to produce.

And his philosophy has remained remarkably consistent.

"I will play as long as the game is fun," he has said time after time. "When I stop having fun, I'll walk away."

He hasn't walked away yet. ∎

(opposite) Many fans don't realize that Favre had come close to losing his starting job in 1993.

Deal of the Century

When Ron Wolf heard the words from Packers team doctor Patrick McKenzie, he couldn't believe it.

It was some surreal dream that Wolf, newly installed as the Packers general manager, was convinced he would awaken from.

Yes, that's it, Wolf thought. I'll pinch myself and wake up and what I heard won't have existed at all.

But it did. It was only too real.

The player he had staked his future with the Packers on had just failed his initial physical with the team. A series of nagging injuries from a bad shoulder to a sore knee had left him something on the order of damaged goods.

Wolf really didn't know what to think or how to react.

He had coveted this young stallion for three years, ever since Wolf was the player personnel director for the New York Jets and Favre was flinging footballs for Southern Mississippi.

"This kid had something I couldn't put my finger on," Wolf said. "But I knew he was going to be special. Don't ask me how I knew, but I knew."

Wolf had begged the Jets to draft Favre in the 1991 draft, but the Atlanta Falcons scooped him up instead. Interestingly enough, Favre had flown so low under the radar in his college career that not even the NFL exec who announced the draft pick to the media and the waiting audience knew what to do.

When Favre's name came to the podium, he was announced as "quarterback, Brett 'Fay-verer.'"

Who knew? Favre had a solid college career but played in a weak conference and was injured much of his senior year, so his draft stock had fallen to the point that he was a second-round pick and the third quarterback taken in the draft—behind Dan McGwire and Todd Marinovich.

Nonetheless, Wolf's disappointment on missing out on Favre was palpable. Wolf saw him as a franchise-altering quarterback. Few others did.

But everything happens for a reason, and circumstances always change, and there may be no better example of that than Ron Wolf.

Barely a year later, Wolf was offered the daunting task of turning the Green Bay Packers franchise around. He was told by team president Bob Harlan that everyone was sick of the years of mediocrity. A storied franchise had fallen into disrepair, and he wanted Wolf to fix it.

To that end, he gave Wolf carte blanche to do

(opposite) "This kid had something I couldn't put my finger on, but I knew he was going to be special. Don't ask me how I knew, but I knew." –Ron Wolf

AP/Wide World

whatever was necessary, spend whatever money he needed to spend, and get whatever tools were required to get the job done.

That was in December 1991. In January, Wolf hired Mike Holmgren as head coach, outdueling several other teams that were also looking for head coaches.

In February, he made the next audacious move—trading a first-round pick in 1992 for Favre, an unproven, unknown player with a funny name.

As a historical footnote, the Falcons used that number-one pick to select another Southern Mississippi player, running back Tony Smith. He lasted three seasons, played little, earned the reputation as a guy who wouldn't play hurt, and was gone from the league the same year Favre was entering the pantheon as one of the NFL's great young quarterbacks.

But that wasn't Wolf's concern. He made the deal he needed to make, and it was time to implement that plan slowly but surely.

Holmgren, the young offensive genius who had studied at the right hand of Bill Walsh, would design the attack that Favre, the young gunslinger,

(opposite) Favre had flown so low under the radar in his college career that not even the NFL executive who announced the draft pick got his name right: He was announced as "quarterback, Brett 'Fay-verer.'" (above) Holmgren was a young offensive genius who used the West Coast scheme.

would eventually run.

It all seemed perfect. Until, of course, the day the bombshell was dropped on Wolf that his prized possession hadn't passed his routine physical.

Wolf had been so confident about his decision to trade for Favre that he hadn't even drawn up language in his contract about any contingency plans if Favre didn't pass his physical exam.

Wolf kept that information under wraps and, indeed, only revealed that fact three years ago after he had long retired from the organization. In fact, Favre wasn't even aware he had flunked.

The solution? It was simple as Wolf saw it.

"I sent him back over for another physical," Wolf recalled with a laugh. "And I said [to the doctors], 'He's going to pass.' And he did. I mean I pinned my career on that guy."

The deal that sent Favre to the Packers for that first-round selection is generally viewed as one of the great lopsided deals not only in pro football, but in sports.

But it didn't look that way at first.

That's because, before any great career can get started, it has to go through what can generously

(opposite) The deal that sent Favre to the Packers for a first-round draft pick is generally viewed as one of the great lopsided deals not only in football, but in sports. (above) Favre did his best work when instinct took over and his terrific arm bailed him out of trouble.

be called "growing pains."

Favre graduated from the football school of Throw It and Pray. He improvised all the time, even in high school when his coach (and father) all but tossed out the playbook because his QB wasn't going to follow it, anyway.

He was best when he wasn't thinking. He did his best work when instinct took over and his terrific arm bailed him out of trouble.

It had always worked for him before, and he saw no reason why it wouldn't in the NFL.

Mike Holmgren was from a different school.

He learned the game the way most coaches did. Even as a young assistant coach in high school, he went to every coaching clinic he could afford to attend. And he would absorb it all.

He knew there was a right way to play and there was the other way, and he decided early on which way he was going to go. That meant if a receiver was supposed to run a 12-yard "out" pattern, it was 12 yards. Not 11 and not 13. He was a stickler for practice, practice, practice, because the only way to get the play right was to know it as well as you knew your own name. That was the way to play. That was

(opposite) Mike Holmgren preached practice and precision as the keys to offensive success. (above) Favre was quick to adapt to his new town and teammates. Getting use to the cold weather would take longer.

the way to practice. It was about precision.

And he preached the so-called "West Coast" offense that he learned as quarterbacks coach and then offensive coordinator of the powerful San Francisco 49ers.

"West Coast" offense was a title every coach who ran it (and there were a lot of them then and even more now) despised. It didn't mean anything. It didn't convey what the offense was supposed to be.

Worse, there was the connotation that the offense was soft. Instead of running two yards for a first down as had often been the case in the past, this offense would use a two-step quarterback drop and a quick pass to gain the yardage.

It was a different way to play the game and, perfected under 49ers' head coach Bill Walsh, it had become effective and successful.

And Holmgren was a true believer in every sense of the word.

It was a foregone conclusion, obviously, that that's what he would run in Green Bay and that's what his new team would buy into. If they didn't, they would play elsewhere.

Into this regimen stepped Favre, who didn't really know what he was stepping into even though he knew it was better than what he was leaving in Atlanta.

Favre wasn't ready his first season, and everyone knew it except Favre. He would sit behind the established Packers' veteran, Don Majkowski, who three years earlier was the chosen one.

But Majkowski's star was already dimming. He had one terrific season, in 1989, as he nearly single-handedly led the Packers to a 10–6 record. But even though they missed the playoffs, the excite-ment was building and coach Lindy Infante was given a new, lucrative contract.

But instead of building on that success, everything began to fall apart. Majkowski took part in a divisive and nasty contract holdout that lasted into the regular season. His opportunity had come and gone.

The Packers went 6–10 in 1990 and tumbled to 4–12 in 1991. That led to Infante's dismissal and Harlan's decision that enough was enough.

Nonetheless, in 1992 Holmgren didn't have much else to work with at quarterback. Majkowski was the veteran and seemed healthy again after a disastrous '91 season. Favre was still in just his second season and had a lot to learn.

Without much choice, Holmgren began his first season in Green Bay with Majkowski as the starter and Favre as his anxious backup.

The plan seemed simple enough. The Packers would suffer through the spasms of growth under Majkowski until Favre proved he was ready. It might be one season, it could be two. But Holmgren wasn't ready to pull the trigger on the young quarterback until he thought he was ready.

But even the best-conceived plans, as Holmgren discovered, sometimes change. And his plans for the Green Bay Packers changed in the blink of an eye. Or more specifically, the snap of a ligament. ∎

(opposite) Without much choice, Holmgren began 1992 with Don Majkowski as the starter and Favre as his anxious backup.

In the Beginning

It's understandable that nearly every Green Bay Packers fan claims to have been in attendance at the Ice Bowl at Lambeau Field or the Packers triumphant Super Bowl XXXI win in New Orleans. And why not? Every fan feels some entitlement and owns some stake in the franchise that they have lived and died with over the decades.

So it was on September 20, 1992. It was a sunny and warm day at Lambeau when the Green Bay Packers took on the Cincinnati Bengals. There was nothing about the game that seemed any different than the ones that had come before. But make no mistake, change was on the way. And today nearly every Packers fan claims to have witnessed in person what happened.

The Packers were 0–2 heading into that game. Green Bay had lost its home opener to the Minnesota Vikings, 23–20, in Mike Holmgren's head-coaching debut.

The next week in Tampa, the Packers were patently awful, falling to the Buccaneers 31–3. That game was noteworthy only for the fact that Favre made his first appearance for the Packers and completed his first-ever NFL pass—to himself. With the game out of reach in the fourth quarter,

Favre had his pass tipped at the line of scrimmage and he instinctively reached up and caught it.

It wasn't the most auspicious beginning. Then again, you have to start somewhere.

There was no doubt Majkowski was still the Packers' starter heading into week three against the Bengals. Majkowski had outperformed Favre in training camp and, by virtue of his experience in the league, also knew the offense better.

But the Packers were 0–2, and nothing seemed as though it had changed much, despite the change in coaches and philosophy.

But midway through the first quarter, Majkowski sprained his left ankle when a Bengals defensive tackle rolled onto him during a play. Majkowski said he heard something pop in the ankle, and as any athlete knows, popping sounds anywhere are rarely a good thing.

As he limped off the field, Holmgren looked at Favre and said simply, "You're in."

It was the first meaningful opportunity in Favre's young career and the beginning of something truly special—though, obviously, no one knew that at the time.

Over the next two-and-a-half quarters, Favre

[opposite] Favre watched from the bench early in his Packers career, but an ankle injury to Don Majkowski would quickly put Favre in charge.

played a game his befuddled head coach had never seen before.

"He had us lined up in formations I'd never seen," a bemused Holmgren would recall later. "He was calling plays we didn't have. He was doing things I couldn't believe."

The story has taken on something of legendary status since, and no doubt even Holmgren was embellishing the tale just a little.

But what was fact was that Favre wasn't very good. He looked like a young quarterback who was out of his element and unsure what to do next. He was sacked five times and fumbled four times as the Packers fell behind 20–10 midway through the fourth quarter.

But what Favre lacked in experience and knowledge, he more than made up for with instinct and moxie.

Favre threw a five-yard touchdown pass to Sterling Sharpe late in the fourth quarter to pull Green Bay to within 20–17 and provide hope.

Then came the stuff of legend. Trailing 23–17, the Packers had the ball on their own 8 with barely a minute to play. Favre then embarked on the first

(opposite) What Favre lacked in experience and knowledge, he more than made up for with instinct and moxie. (above) "He's not a quarterback. He plays the position, but he plays the game more like a linebacker." –James Campen

of what would be a trunkful of fourth-quarter comebacks for his team.

It wasn't easy and it wasn't pretty, but somehow Favre maneuvered the Packers down to the Bengals 35 with 19 seconds to play.

On a play called "2 Jet All Go," four wide receivers took off downfield and one of them, a journeyman wideout named Kitrick Taylor, who had stepped in for the injured Sharpe, was open down the right sideline.

A Favre pump-fake (which would become a major part of his repertoire) froze a Bengals' safety, and Favre rifled a throw in Taylor's general direction. Favre has always said he closed his eyes and waited for the reaction—and he heard the one he was waiting for.

Taylor made the catch in stride and scored the touchdown that gave Green Bay its first win of the season.

Favre was so thrilled he ran around the field looking for someone, anyone to hug. He eventually found starting offensive lineman Ron Hallstrom, whom he head-butted, opening a gash on Favre's forehead.

After the game, teammates marveled at how their young quarterback had performed.

One comment, from veteran center James Campen, was especially telling.

"He's not a quarterback," Campen said. "He plays the position, but he plays the game more like a linebacker."

Campen, having moved on from his playing days, is a Packers offensive line coach today while Favre continues to do what he's always been doing.

After the game, Holmgren, not given to much hyperbole then, said simply, "If Brett can stay healthy, he will be the cornerstone of our football team for many years to come."

Even he didn't know how true that observation was.

What transpired that day was something every Packers fan remembers now. It was Favre's first comeback victory. It was his first win. It was the first demonstration that he was the guy to lead this team. In a game where he played basically on guts and instinct, he completed 22 of 39 passes for 289 yards and two scores.

And, really, it was the first indication to Packers fans, Holmgren, and Wolf that the future had begun. Perhaps it was sooner than anyone had anticipated, but it had started.

It's likely that even if Majkowski's ankle injury wasn't that serious (which it was), the veteran QB wouldn't have found his way back into the lineup.

This was Favre's team now.

The joke among the media that covered the Packers was that Holmgren wanted Favre in the lineup so badly, the Packers coach would have fallen on Majkowski's ankle if the Bengals hadn't.

The next week, Favre started his first game for the Packers—a streak that continues to this day—against the Pittsburgh Steelers.

But there was more to that season than simply a great comeback win. It was a season that set the tone for nearly everything that would occur for the Packers over the next 15 years.

Favre guided the Packers to a 9–5 record (9–7 overall) that season under his leadership and threw for 3,227 yards and 18 touchdowns. But the numbers don't really say anything.

What he did that year was show the rest of the

(opposite) "If Brett can stay healthy, he will be the cornerstone of our football team for many years to come." – Mike Holmgren

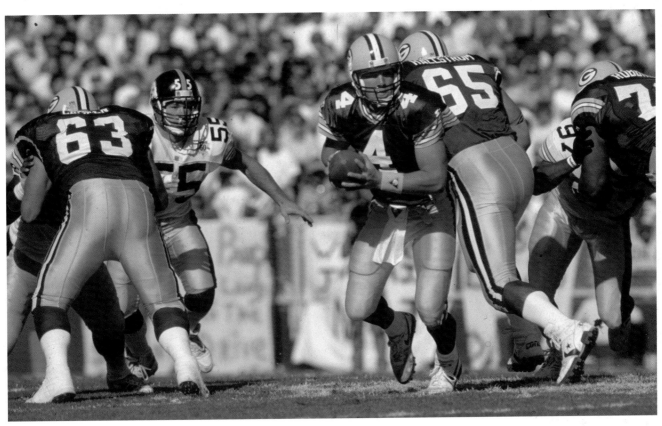

NFL that a new day was dawning for the Packers. Here was a kid who wasn't afraid of anything. He had the skills and the temperament to take this team a long way.

He would play horrifically at times, including a three-interception explosion against the New York Giants. But he never let the bad plays or the lousy games impact him. He had a gift for shaking off poor plays and moving on to the next.

A perfect example that season came in a November 15 game against the tough Philadelphia Eagles at Milwaukee County Stadium.

The Eagles featured perhaps the toughest defense in the NFL those days, and it was led by the incomparable sack-master, defensive end Reggie White.

Indeed, White introduced himself to the new pup when he hit Favre so hard in the second quarter that he separated Favre's left shoulder. Favre said of all the injuries he's suffered over the years, that one hurt the most.

But he played through it and completed 23 of 33 passes for 275 yards and two touchdowns as the Packers came from behind for the 27–24 win.

In another piece of Packers lore, that game also had lasting significance.

Reggie White was so impressed with Favre's grit and toughness, especially leading his team to the

(opposite) Favre showed the rest of the NFL that a new day was dawning for the Packers in 1992. (above) Favre's teammates appreciated his mental and physical toughness.

win after an injury like that, that he filed it away for future reference.

That memory popped up again after that season when White, then the subject of the most frantic free-agency battle the NFL had ever seen, was looking for a new place to play.

The high-profile Washington Redskins and San Francisco 49ers seemingly had the money and the prestige to make the best offer, but Green Bay decided to dip its toe into the pool, as well. The Packers' monetary offer was comparable and, indeed, a little better than some of the others, but there was also the idea of playing in Green Bay.

Back then, Green Bay still had the stigma of an NFL outpost where players went when they couldn't cut it anywhere else. But that attitude was slowly starting to change, thanks in large part to Favre and what he was bringing to the franchise.

Eventually, White decided that Green Bay was the place for him, and one of the reasons, among several he cited, was the way Favre played in Milwaukee. He saw in Favre the quarterback who could take him, and the Packers, to the Super Bowl. "I want to be part of that," White said.

Favre has always downplayed his role in luring White to Green Bay. Indeed, most people look at the staggering offer (four years, $19 million, which was astronomical back then) as the biggest reason. And, very likely, it was the driving reason.

But four years later, when Favre and White teamed up to bring the Vince Lombardi Trophy to Green Bay, the two men hugged at midfield of the Superdome in New Orleans.

"We did it," Favre said.

"Thanks," White said.

All of that began to be built that first ragged season when no one knew what to expect from this young quarterback and the quarterback didn't really know what he was doing.

The Packers finished 9–7 in 1992, just missing out on the playoffs after losing to the Minnesota Vikings in the season finale. But just the fact that Green Bay was even in position to challenge for a playoff spot satisfied a lot of people.

Favre was the fifth-rated quarterback in the NFC that season, with his 3,227 passing yards and 18 touchdowns. For his performance, he earned his first invitation to the Pro Bowl. It would not be his last.

But while many people were thrilled with the Packers season, Holmgren and Favre were not. They had made strides together as coach and pupil, and the team had responded. But there was a long way to go.

Hard work and perfection were never anything new to Favre. He had learned that from the time he was old enough to pick up a football.

In fact, go back to Kiln, Mississippi, and, more specifically, the family homestead in a wondrously named place called Stinking Springs.

It was place literally on the edge of a bayou, and whenever Favre would take friends down to his home, they would shake their heads in amazement.

Center Frank Winters, a kid from New Jersey who grew up across the river from New York City, went down there often and was always amazed by what he saw.

"The alligators would come right up to the porch," Winters would say, as if he still couldn't believe it.

(opposite) Favre had a gift for shaking off poor plays and moving on to the next.

But that's where Favre came from. That's what he knew. That background made him what he would ultimately become.

In one of the more surreal moments prior to Super XXXI in New Orleans, a media bus trip was scheduled to drive the one hour to Kiln. That's where reporters could talk to residents and get a sense of what Brett Favre meant to everyone.

It didn't go exactly as planned, as most residents really didn't have much to say. He was Brett. He had always been Brett and he always would be. Besides, by that point, most of the people in the area had grown used to his career as an NFL star.

But what everyone also knew was that whatever Brett Favre had learned over the years—whether it was tenacity or pig-headedness—it came from his folks, Irvin and Bonita.

There was something in the Favre-family DNA that refused to accept defeat. Even as far back as elementary school, his dad could see the aggressiveness and tenacity in his son.

Brett Favre was always one of the town's top athletes, whether it was football or baseball. But he wasn't so spectacular that he dominated other kids.

(opposite) As Favre carried the Packers to national prominence, media attention began to grow for the young star. (above) Favre and Mike Holmgren quickly built a winning rapport.

AP/Wide World

He was a terrific athlete but in a way that made it seem as though other athletes could at least compete against him. He wasn't a big guy, and as anyone who had watched him throw a football could attest, he wasn't schooled in the quarterback arts.

But he had that arm, that incredible thunderbolt of an arm. No one could touch him in terms of pure velocity.

So, of course, at Hancock High what did his coach (and dad) do? He ran the veer offense, a predominantly running offense. But Favre ran it and ran it well, because that's what he was required to do.

It was a competitive, complicated relationship between Irvin and Brett. Irvin was an accomplished athlete in his youth, and he passed that competitiveness on to his kids, especially Brett.

Indeed, the two competed at everything and neither gave an inch.

Because he played deep in the Mississippi bayou and never really got a chance to show his arm strength, Favre wasn't highly recruited out of high school. His only real offer, in fact, came from nearby Southern Mississippi, a program that, not unlike the Green Bay Packers, was trying to get some national notoriety.

(opposite) In his early appearances, Favre looked like a young quarterback who was out of his element and unsure what to do next. (above) No one told Favre that becoming a star would be easy, for life and football had already become one battle after another.

The coaches were intrigued by the youngster, but in another story that has become part of the legend, Favre started the season as the number-seven (and last) quarterback on the USM depth chart.

But Favre amazed the coaches with the sheer velocity of his throws. Even as a 17-year-old freshman, Favre had that certain something, with his teammates and in the huddle, that coaches always look for but rarely find.

Indeed, he was thrown into the deep end of the pool that first year as he ran the USM's number-two offense against the number-one defense—just to see what he could do.

He was so impressive in that stint that some of the defensive players started chanting, "Elway, Elway, Elway," in tribute to the game's top quarterback at the time.

Jeff Bower took over as the Golden Eagles' offensive coordinator in 1988, and that's where Favre began to blossom. In 1988 he threw for 2,271 yards and 16 touchdowns as Southern Mississippi posted a 10–2 record and beat Texas–El Paso in the Independence Bowl. In 1989, the Eagles slumped to 5–6 but Favre still threw for 2,588 yards (still a school record) and 14 touchdowns.

Favre was perched to have a spectacular senior season that figured to translate into, very likely, a first-round selection in the 1990 NFL draft.

But the roadblocks that would torment Favre nearly every time he turned around showed up again in the summer of his senior season.

On the night of July 14, 1990, Favre was returning from an outing near home when, apparently, an oncoming car blinded him with his headlights. Favre's car veered off the road and smashed into a tree. His car was totaled, and to this day, Favre still doesn't remember what happened.

He was taken to the hospital where he was originally diagnosed with a bruised liver and a concussion.

Initially, he was released from the hospital and told to simply rest up and let the bumps and bruises heal. But soon it became obvious that there was something else wrong.

Instead of the stomach pain from the accident easing up and going away, the pain got worse and even for Favre, it was time to see what was wrong.

The diagnosis was that the original stomach injury had caused an intestinal blockage that was causing a problem in his small intestine. Favre went into immediate surgery and 30 inches of his small intestine were removed.

There are many in the family who feel that Brett's eventual problems with painkillers might have started there as he recuperated from the painful surgery.

And while Favre was told he would make a full recovery, he was warned to take it easy. He could resume his football career, but it would take some time. He missed Southern Mississippi's season-opener and, indeed, was told to wait two more weeks before returning to the field.

But looming next for USM was powerful Alabama, and it was a game Favre was determined to play in.

Though Golden Eagles head coach Curley Hallman was reluctant to let his recovering quarterback play, Favre had a way of making everyone believe he knew what he was doing. And finally, he was allowed to play.

The result was predictable. Favre's appearance in

(opposite) The 1992 season was one that set the tone for nearly everything that would occur for the Packers over the next 15 years.

the huddle and his innate leadership skills inspired his teammates. Favre didn't post spectacular numbers, as he completed 9 of 17 passes for 125 yards, but as is often the case with Favre, the numbers rarely tell the story.

Just having him in the game, withstanding Alabama's withering defense, was all the Golden Eagles needed. The result was a stunning 27–24 upset of the Crimson Tide.

That game, and the way Favre played through it, caught the attention of the national media who otherwise probably couldn't have found the university with a map. In fact it was that year that Ron Wolf's interest in Favre was truly piqued.

Later that season, Favre's stock continued to rise as the upstart USM went to Auburn and pulled off another upset, with Favre throwing for 207 yards and two crucial touchdowns.

Favre's final season at Southern Mississippi wasn't anything special statistically, but he had made his point. He had shown the grit and determination that would last him his entire career.

There were questions about his size, his awful mechanics, his questionable decision-making. But this guy was a warrior, and every team in the NFL knew you could never have enough of them.

No one knew if he could be an NFL quarterback. But it was worth finding out. ∎

(opposite) One of the factors that helped make Reggie White a Packer was the toughness and resiliency Favre showed when White was still playing in Philadelphia. (above) Ty Detmer and Favre were the backup quarterbacks for the Packers at the start of 1992.

Though never a big threat scrambling with the ball, Favre has always been able to move around well enough to elude tacklers.

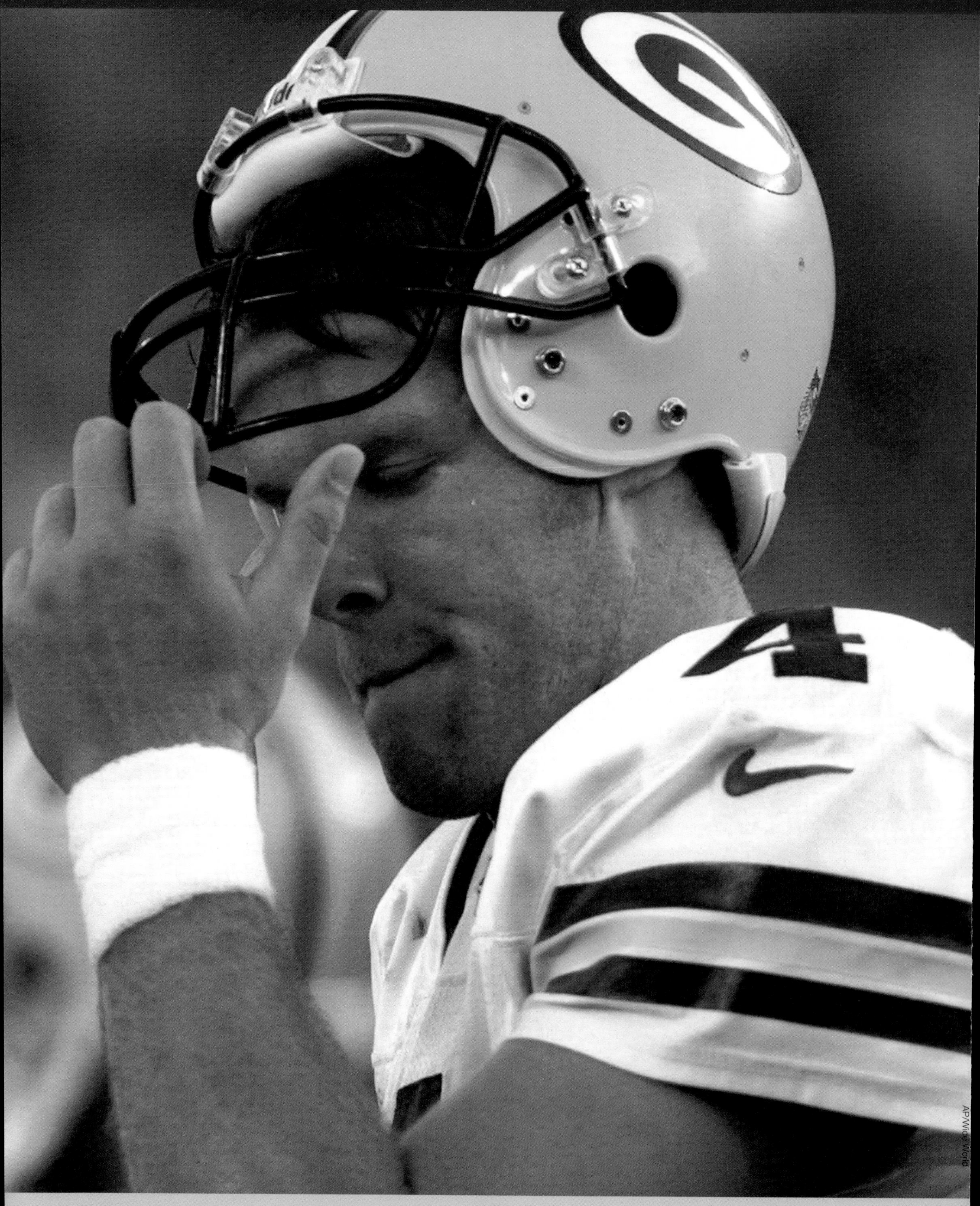

AP/Wide World

Growing Pains

No one said it was going to be easy.

And certainly no one had to say that to Brett Favre, for whom life and football had already been one battle after another. But whether it was proving himself in high school or proving himself in college or, perhaps most important of all, proving himself to his imposing father, Favre had always found a way to make it happen.

The NFL, he figured, would be just one more challenge.

He knew he'd get his chance in the NFL, but what concerned him was how much of an opportunity he'd get and how much baggage he might have to carry, especially after a senior season that wasn't what anyone expected.

Keep in mind that, after his junior season, there was even talk that Favre might be a Heisman Trophy candidate. It was never all that serious, except around the Hattiesburg campus, but the fact remained that Favre had made enough people notice him.

All that hype and all those expectations went up in smoke after Favre wrapped his car around that tree that fateful July night.

It was now about recognition and survival for Favre. He knew he could play at the next level, and all he was looking for, as were hundreds of other prospective players, was the chance.

Far from Hattiesburg, the wheels were turning in Ron Wolf's mind. His interest in Favre was known around the league, but no one really knew how serious it was. Indeed, some of the personnel directors around the league wondered why the NFL veteran was so enamored of a quarterback who played at a school not exactly known for churning out NFL-caliber players.

But originally, even Wolf wasn't sure he was looking at anyone special. That's because Wolf did what he was expected to do—he watched film from Favre's senior season, after the car accident.

Alone in the film room, Wolf thought he was looking at just another good college quarterback. He made the plays, he did what he was expected to do, and he was a winner. That was clear.

But in Wolf's mind, a franchise quarterback, a first-rounder, should be something special. He wanted to see something jumping off the film, and it just wasn't there. Ready to dismiss Favre as a nice player and little more, he was stopped by USM assistant coach Thamus Coleman. In what turned out to be a stroke of genius, Coleman suggested

(opposite) Favre knew he'd get his chance in the NFL, but what concerned him was how much of an opportunity he'd get.

that Wolf look at film from Favre's junior season. With little else to do on a quiet afternoon in southern Mississippi, Wolf agreed.

That's when he saw what he needed to see. In Wolf's view, this kid was the kind of special player every team needs. He went so far as to say that Favre might be the steal of the draft.

Favre didn't hurt his case with some exceptional postseason all-star game performances, including throwing for 218 yards, throwing for one score and running for another in the East-West game in California. Favre was named the game's co-offensive MVP, and Wolf was there to see it.

If he'd had any doubt about what he'd seen from Favre in the film room, it was gone now. Wolf left the game convinced that Favre was the best quarterback in the draft.

Wolf went so far as to convince Jets general manager Dick Steinberg that Favre was their man and that they needed to do whatever they could to get him. Unfortunately for the Jets, they didn't have a first-round pick and so had an agonizing wait to see if their top player would still be around for the second round.

The Jets had the 34th selection in the draft; 32 other selections had been made, and Favre was still there. But on pick number 33, Favre was taken by the Atlanta Falcons.

Wolf was crushed. The Jets ended up selecting Louisville quarterback Browning Nagle, whom Falcons head coach Jerry Glanville had favored in the first place.

Favre, of course, had no idea of the machinations going on in New York and how badly Wolf coveted him. Instead, Favre was thrilled to have been drafted by the Falcons. The only thing that would have been better for him was going to his favorite team as a kid, the New Orleans Saints. But he was staying in the South, and his family could see him play.

But that enthusiasm was tempered soon after, when the Falcons traded for veteran Billy Joe Tolliver to serve as backup for starter Chris Miller. That meant Favre was, at best, the number-three quarterback.

He felt slighted and was angry. He wouldn't even get a chance to compete for the backup role, and Favre's hurt feelings began to seep into his attitude.

He wasn't a great teammate and he admits that now. He never got along with Glanville, a free spirit in his own right who had little tolerance for Favre and his antics.

In the book *Brett Favre: Huck Finn Grows Up*, written in 1996 by Steve Cameron, Glanville recalls his view of the rookie.

"All he did was drink beer and eat chicken wings for a year," Glanville said. "He looked like the Pillsbury Doughboy. He's the only guy I've ever coached in 31 years who missed the team picture, and that didn't sit too good with me. With Brett I'd put numbers on the board for his excuses. I used to tell him not to make up excuses; just give me a number. I didn't want to listen to it."

It wasn't the ideal way to start an NFL career, and Favre knew it, but as he often said, "I really didn't care."

He was disillusioned, angry, frustrated, and he wasn't getting a chance to play. His only outlet on game days was in warm-ups, when he'd heave a ball as high into the upper deck of a stadium as he could.

Asked if he'd get a chance to play one game, Favre

[opposite] Ron Wolf went so far as to say that Favre might be the steal of the 1991 Draft.

was told by Glanville, "Only if the other quarterbacks on the team get in a train wreck."

It was a miserable year for Favre, even though the Falcons did earn a playoff berth. Favre threw just five passes that season, completed none. But Favre chalked up the year to experience and vowed to make 1992 a better season. He had been told by the Falcons that he remained a valuable part of their future plans and they had no intention of cutting or trading him.

But Glanville never liked Favre—personally or professionally. The two men mixed like the proverbial oil and water, and that off-season Glanville made it clear he wanted to get rid of the turbulent quarterback.

And the wheels moved even faster.

Wolf had moved on from the Jets to take over the role of rebuilding the Green Bay Packers. And Favre was never far from his thoughts.

Among his rebuilding projects was finding the right coach and the right quarterback. He had the coach in Mike Holmgren, and he genuinely believed Favre was his quarterback.

He had some awareness of what Favre had, or had not, done in Atlanta, but he didn't care.

Wolf figured if he put him in the right situation with the right guidance, the kid would thrive.

"I remember Ron and I went to New York to watch the Falcons play at the end of the 1991 season," Packers president Bob Harlan said. "Ron put his stuff down in the press box, and he said 'I going to go down and watch this kid for the Falcons warm up. If he's still got the same arm, I'm going to trade for him.' Ron came back up and said, 'I'm going to get him. Is that okay?' I told him, 'You do what you need to do. This is your team now.'"

It was a straight-up deal, a rarity in the NFL. The Packers gave up their number-one pick the following April for this young, untested, essentially unknown quarterback.

NFL observers were bemused, and Packers fans, who had been beaten down over the years by bad deals, bad decisions, and bad players, were furious.

But Holmgren, at least outwardly, supported the deal.

In the press conference announcing the move, Holmgren said. "When you get a chance to get a quarterback that you think can be a great one, you do it."

Whether Holmgren really believed it or not is another question. But as much as Wolf was tying his future to the quarterback, Holmgren was doing it, too, but to a far greater degree.

After all, Holmgren would have the day-to-day responsibility of teaching this kid how to play the game the way the Packers wanted it played now. Would he listen to his new coach, who was already known to possess a volcanic temper and had little patience for stupid mistakes?

Would he rise above the negative publicity and thrive, or if things got tough, would he go back to his beer-and-chicken-wings ways?

He went to Green Bay, and it was like he had stepped into another world. He knew as much about Wisconsin as he did about the surface of Neptune. The Packers had shown no interest in him during the '91 draft, and that had been just fine with him. Indeed, many college players from the South would cringe when they learned they had been drafted by the Packers.

It wasn't so much the team or the situation,

(opposite) Favre would quickly form a bond with his receivers in Green Bay, including Sterling Sharpe.

though. It was that weather. That damn cold weather that seemed to set in by October and wouldn't leave until May. You were cold all the time, and the people who lived there—those lunatic Packers fans—reveled in the stuff. Players would look up into the stands—on the coldest days many of them had ever felt—and they'd see fans who were naked from the waist up and loving it.

These were people you couldn't help but like, but many players often wondered about their sanity.

And even through the years of staggering mediocrity on the field, those fans were always there. They supported the Packers through thick and thin and everything in between.

It was into this situation that Favre stepped. He was no different than the other players from the South. He hated the cold but he loved football, so he would make the best of the situation. What choice did he have?

Ironically, as the years rolled by and Favre's legend grew, his record in cold weather would prove to be one of his proudest accomplishments.

In the first 29 home games of Favre's career in which the temperature was 34 degrees or below, he never lost a game. Through the 2006 season, he was 40–5 when the temperature was at or below freezing at Lambeau.

It was a statistic he knew about and enjoyed but frankly didn't understand.

"I hate the stuff," he'd say.

Of course, a lot of it had to do with the fact that he played on some awfully good teams, so it really didn't matter what the temperature was or what was falling from the sky. Dominance was dominance, and it knew no barometric pressure.

But in those first three years in Green Bay, there was no dominance. There was no home-field advantage. There was no feeling that, by just stepping on the field, the Packers had an advantage over everyone they played.

This was a franchise starting from scratch, and everyone, including Favre, knew it.

Favre stepped into a situation that, as it turned out, was ideal for him. He hooked up with hungry young players who also wanted to make names for themselves. They all had clean slates, and whatever had occurred in the past no longer mattered.

In 1991, the Packers had sunk back to the depths of the mediocrity they thought they had escaped from.

By the end of that season, Blair Kiel was the quarterback, the leading rusher Darrell Thompson. The defense was demoralized and decimated, and the offense close to nonexistent. Lindy Infante, who two years earlier was hailed in a fan poll as the best coach in team history (and earned a contract extension that Harlan regretted almost immediately) had lost control of the team and he knew it.

So when Ron Wolf was hired as the first general manager since Vince Lombardi in November, Infante knew his days were numbered.

He was right as Wolf fired Infante the day after the season and, in an intense war with four other NFL teams, signed Holmgren as his head coach.

Around him, Holmgren assembled a young, talented staff, several of whom would go on to become head coaches in their own right. They included the likes of Steve Mariucci, Andy Reid, Dick Jauron, Ray Rhodes, and a young kid named Jon Gruden.

It was just what Favre needed to help his transi-

(opposite) Favre chalked up the 1991 season to experience and vowed to make 1992 a better season.

tion. And all along, even Holmgren wouldn't say it at the time, he knew Favre was his quarterback of the future.

But first there was the transition from wild kid to controlled pro quarterback. It was not an easy journey.

Favre bristled at Holmgren's tough, regimented style. His players would do it his way, and Favre, like a rebellious teenager, would always want to know why.

On more occasions than either could count, Favre would zip a pass between three defenders in practice, and Holmgren would erupt. It was a bad, dangerous play, said Holmgren. But I completed the pass, said Favre.

Once he took over the job in early 1992, the course work was accelerated for Favre. This was his team, and it was time to move forward with the plan.

Harlan still remembers the first time he met Favre, a player he knew nothing about, but in whom his new general manager had complete confidence.

The Packers were in Tampa in 1992 and were going through a light workout the day before the game.

"Now I had never met him before," Harlan recalled. "I'm standing on the field just watching, and here he comes jogging by and he says, 'How ya doin', Bob?' Just like that. Now I have a problem with people calling me 'Mr. Harlan,' anyway. But here comes Brett, and he's already made up his mind that I'm 'Bob.' And I thought to myself, 'I'm going to like this guy.'"

Yes, he was likeable. Everyone knew that. But he was stubborn and so convinced of his own ability that no one could tell him otherwise. That would lead to conflict after conflict with Holmgren.

And while the war of wills raged behind the scenes, Holmgren kept up the public face that all was well with the development of his young quarterback.

Favre may well have been lulled into a false sense of security after that first season. The game didn't exactly come easily to him, but as he led the Packers to a 9–7 season and earned a spot in the Pro Bowl, he may have thought that this NFL thing wasn't so tough after all.

But 1993 was a watershed for Favre. He came in hailed as one of the top young quarterbacks in the game, and he did nothing to tarnish that image by throwing for 264 yards and two touchdowns in a season-opening win over the Los Angeles Rams.

Over the next four games, mortality began to creep into Favre's game. He threw for more than 200 yards just once in that span and threw seven interceptions compared to just three touchdowns.

Suddenly, what had come easily was now a struggle for the sharpshooter. And as the mistakes piled up, Holmgren's legendary impatience began to sharpen. He was willing to put up with some mistakes, that was the by-product of a young player. But what Holmgren couldn't abide were the same mistakes over and over.

What kept the situation from boiling over into a major conflict was the presence of quarterbacks coach Steve Mariucci. No one truly understood what Mariucci meant to that relationship between Favre and Holmgren. He was the peace-keeper, the proverbial "good cop" to Holmgren's "bad cop."

When Holmgren fulminated about another Favre miscue, pushing the quarterback to the edge of sanity, Mariucci would step in.

He'd take Favre to the side and tell him to relax and

(opposite) NFL observers were bemused and Packers fans, who had been beaten down over the years by bad deals, bad decisions, and bad players, were furious over the trade for Favre.

not let Holmgren get to him.

"You're the guy," Mariucci said, even at those times when he really wasn't sure that that was the case.

Mariucci knew all about the Packers and what they meant to the community. He grew up in the Upper Peninsula of Michigan, a huge Packers fan from the time he was a kid. So when he got the chance to join the Packers staff, the easygoing Mariucci gravitated to Favre right away.

He was a quarterbacks coach in name only, in some respects. Holmgren ran the show on the offense, from calling the plays to making sure Favre followed his progressions. Mariucci was there to keep everyone from killing each other. He and Favre became fast friends and remain so even today.

When Mariucci left the Packers after the 1995 season to become head coach at the University of California, there were many who wondered if Favre would take a step back. Instead, he was the one who insisted "Mooch" go after the job. With the quarterback's blessing, Mariucci did just that.

In the ensuing years, when there was coaching upheaval either with the Packers or Mariucci, there was always talk that Favre's favorite coach would return.

The rumors were especially strong late in the 1998 season when it was clear Holmgren was looking for a way out of Green Bay and Mariucci was struggling as head coach of the San Francisco 49ers.

Those two teams met in the NFC playoffs and many "experts" figured if the Packers beat the 'Niners again, Mariucci was gone and Holmgren would take his place.

It didn't happen. The 49ers won an epic battle, Mariucci stayed on, and Holmgren moved on to the Seattle Seahawks.

Talk surfaced again in 2005 when Mike Sherman was fired as the Packers' coach. Who would take his place? Mariucci, who was out of coaching, was a name that kept popping up, and he never said much to dispute it.

That never happened, either. But Favre and Mariucci remain close friends, and maybe that's the way it should be.

But in 1993, he was as valuable a person as anyone Favre knew at the time.

Favre eventually righted himself that season, but his numbers weren't eye-popping.

After his four-game skid, the Packers had a bye week. He returned to throw for 268 yards and four touchdowns in a 37–14 win over Tampa Bay, and if his confidence had been shaken, it wasn't any longer.

It was a season that would prove to be typical of Favre's career.

He went down to the Superdome and led the Packers to an improbable come-from-behind win over the Saints. He struggled all game long against Tampa Bay, eliciting boos at one stretch from the Lambeau faithful, until he led a final drive that resulted in a game-winning touchdown pass to Sterling Sharpe. After the score, he sprinted to the nearest sideline and held up both arms in triumph.

The next week, he completed a new team-record 36 passes for 402 yards against the Chicago Bears. But he also threw three interceptions, two of which were returned for touchdowns.

But he and the Packers did enough to scratch out a 9–7 record and earn their first playoff berth since 1982.

And it was there that Favre etched another spot in

(opposite) Favre and his teammates finally started heading in the right direction in 1993.

his quickly lengthening list of improbable events.

In a wild-card playoff game January 8 against the Detroit Lions in the Silverdome, Favre was truly awful. Every bad habit that had plagued him his entire career seemed to show up that day. But when it mattered most, he was at his best. Again.

Trailing 24–21 in the final minute of the game, Favre faced a second down and 20 from the Lions' 40. Favre was flushed out of the pocket and rolled to his left. He saw Sharpe heading down the right sideline and he heaved a pass across his body that hit Sharpe all by himself in the end zone for the winning score.

It was crazy, ridiculous, unheard of. But it had happened. Somehow the Packers won on a day when he wasn't very good until he had to be.

The next week, the Packers were taken to school by the Dallas Cowboys, though Favre played well enough, throwing two touchdowns in a 27–17 loss.

It was another step in the process. Holmgren knew that. He saw his young quarterback grow up over the course of a sometimes troubling season, and he knew it would pay dividends down the road.

It may be too simplistic to say that the seeds of the Green Bay Packers' NFL dominance, and Brett Favre's emergence as the game's best quarterback five years running, were planted in the 1994 season. Then again, maybe it isn't.

So much happened that season to the Packers, and to Favre, that had never happened before, that it was hard for even the most casual fan to not see something special was happening.

It was a perfect progression since Holmgren had taken over as head coach. He had nearly remade the entire roster from his first days on the job. He had

taken a forlorn program and turned it around immediately. It went 9–7 his first year and barely missed the playoffs. It went 9–7 again in 1993 and reached the second round of the playoffs. Now it was 1994, and all the pieces were falling into place.

It was time to take the next step, and the man to make that happen, obviously, was Brett Favre.

Along with the natural ability Favre had already displayed, he was now developing into a quarterback who could think and process information in a split second.

He had two full years in Mike Holmgren's complex offense, and he knew it almost a well as the coach did.

One of the highlights of the week before games was Mariucci's rapid-fire quizzing of the quarterbacks. Mariucci would throw out the situation, and the quarterbacks—including Favre, Ty Detmer, and Mark Brunell (both of whom would become NFL starters elsewhere)—had to come up with the perfect answer. It was work and it was tedium, and thanks to Favre, it also became a bit of a farce.

He would punctuate discussions with loud, explosive farts that would break up everyone, including Mariucci.

But the important thing was that every time Favre was put on the spot, he would come up with the right answer.

It was the season when, some evidence to the contrary, Favre grew up.

The Packers sputtered early that season, losing four of their first seven games, including a disastrous loss in Minnesota when Favre was knocked from the game with a hip injury. It was the first time in his Packers tenure that he'd had to leave a

(opposite) Favre stepped into a situation that, as it turned out, was ideal for him.

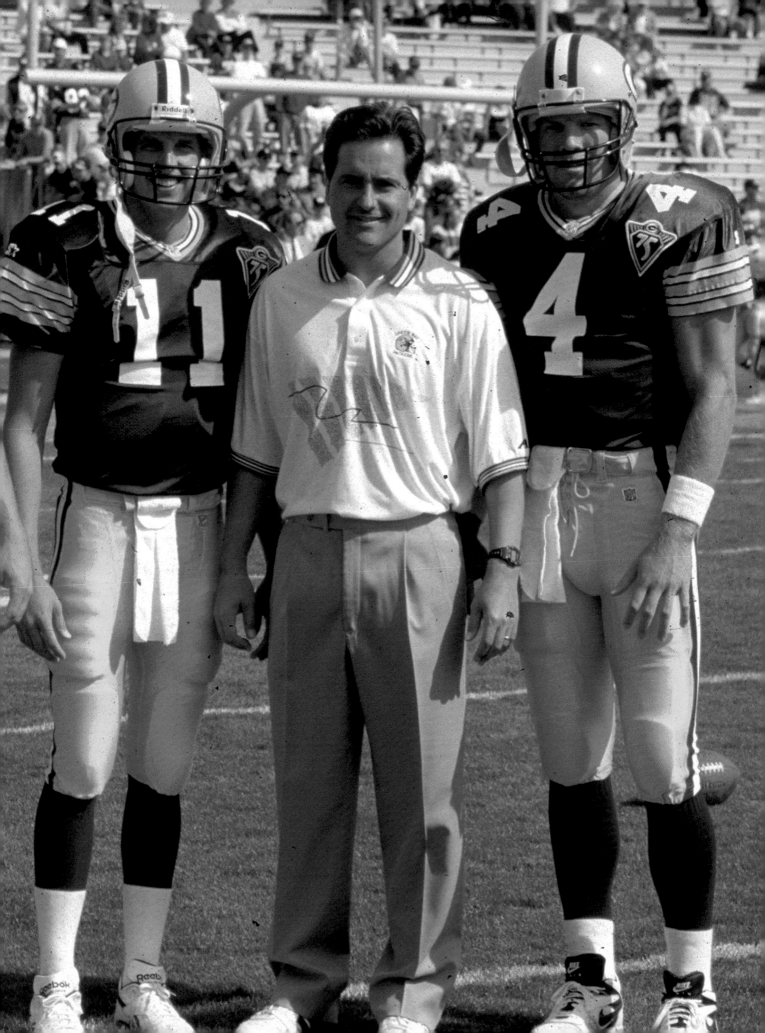

game without finishing.

The following week, they played the Chicago Bears in a fearsome Monday night downpour at Soldier Field.

But Favre managed the game in ways he never really had before. Knowing the conditions were horrendous, he threw just 15 passes and completed six for 82 yards and one touchdown. But the Packers won, and the relief was palpable.

In the eight games that followed, Favre threw 23 touchdown passes and just seven interceptions, and the Packers won five of their last eight.

But the poor start had put the Packers in danger of missing the playoffs for the second time in three years. Green Bay's goal in the final two weeks was to win to have any shot at getting to the postseason.

In another "Favre Moment" on December 18 against the Atlanta Falcons, the Packers again relied on their leader. The Packers were playing their final game at Milwaukee County Stadium, a quaint but wholly unacceptable modern NFL venue.

The Packers needed to beat the Falcons to keep any playoff hope alive, and they seemed to have failed the test, trailing 17–14 with just under two minutes.

"I remember Brett walked into the huddle and looked completely calm," tight end Mark Chmura said at the time. "He knew we were going to win."

Favre then led the Packers on a 67-yard drive down County Stadium's torn-up turf. He completed six of nine passes on the drive, including one decisive fourth-down conversion.

Then, with 14 seconds left, Favre rolled right and dove into the end zone from nine yards out for the winning score. The place exploded.

Team president Bob Harlan recalls the moment,

oh, so well.

"It was my decision to leave Milwaukee, and for safety reasons, the police in both Green Bay and Milwaukee were concerned with me going to the game," he said. "So they agreed to take me and my wife out of the stadium with six minutes to play just to make sure there wouldn't be any problems. So the police got her and they got me and they put us in our car and sent us on our way. I remember listening to the game on the radio and I was so nervous. So when I heard that Brett dove into the end zone, I almost drove off the road. That was just unbelievable. I had to get home and watch replays of it. I think I've watched that play more than any other."

The following week, Favre threw for 291 yards and three scores as the Packers went to Tampa and routed the Buccaneers, cementing a playoff berth.

Green Bay again beat Detroit in the first round of the playoffs and were pounded by the Cowboys in the second round. But another step was complete.

Favre set a club record with 363 completions. He fired 33 touchdown passes and just 14 interceptions, 10 fewer than the season before.

He also had three 3,000-yard passing seasons in his three years in Green Bay. Most important, he was the unquestioned leader of a young, growing, improving franchise that needed only to figure out how to get home-field advantage, and how to beat the Dallas Cowboys, to advance even further.

A new season would lead to new hope. ■

(opposite) Ty Detmer, Steve Mariucci, and Favre worked to bring the Packers respectability at the quarterback position.

Favre walks dejectedly back to the sidelines after the Packers' 38-27 loss to the Dallas Cowboys in the NFC Championship game on January 14, 1996.

Super Times

The Green Bay Packers were becoming the trendy new NFL franchise. The Cowboys and 49ers were slamming away at each other for NFC supremacy, but the Packers were lurking just under the radar, ready for their shot to knock off the kings.

Three years of practically nonstop improvement had left the Packers players, coaches, and fans feeling pretty good about themselves. It was just a matter of time, they all figured.

But the NFL has a funny way of evening the playing field when least expected. In the 1995 season opener, the Packers figured to take care of the Rams, a struggling franchise that was no match for Green Bay, at the suddenly invincible confines of Lambeau Field.

But the Packers ran into a dose of reality that warm day as Favre was intercepted three times; he was harassed from the pocket all day, and the Packers were beaten.

So much for great expectations.

If nothing else, that loss served to refocus the Packers, and they proceeded to rip off five wins in their next six games. But the roller coaster was just getting started.

In a November 5 loss to the Minnesota Vikings in, of course, the Metrodome, Favre, for the second straight year, was knocked from the game. This time it was with a badly sprained left ankle.

After the game, the usually gregarious Favre was silent. He balanced himself on crutches and his foot hung limply. Asked if his quarterback would play the following Sunday in a key matchup against Chicago, Holmgren had no answer.

What followed was a week of football intrigue, misdirection, and uncertainty rarely seen anymore.

For the first time since his arrival, Holmgren closed practice to the media. He had a plan for what was going to happen, but he didn't want anyone to know about it.

By Wednesday, he was still unsure if Favre would play. To make matters worse, backup Ty Detmer had broken his thumb in the Vikings game and was unavailable. And number-three quarterback, T.J. Rubley, who had enraged his coach with an ill-advised audible that led to the loss in Minnesota, was so deep in the doghouse, no one could find him.

Holmgren was so desperate, he signed former 49ers quarterback Bob Gagliano, who had retired and hadn't thrown a pass in three seasons. But he knew Holmgren's offense, and what choice was there?

(opposite) Three years of practically nonstop improvement had left the Packers players, coaches, and fans feeling pretty good about themselves.

Favre didn't practice all week, but come Sunday he told Holmgren he could go. He had the ankle wrapped so tightly that it was as hard as a cast, and he hobbled onto the field.

What followed was another moment to put in the Favre archives.

With no mobility and no practice time, Favre stood in the pocket and carved up the Bears for 336 yards and five touchdowns in the 35–28 win. It is still Favre's only five-touchdown performance.

He said the injury forced him to stand, survey the field, and deliver balls he had never had to throw before.

The next week, Favre's ankle was only marginally better, but no one doubted he'd play in Cleveland. The best part of that game was the verbal jousting between Favre and the Browns' wide receiver, Andre Rison, who called Favre a "hayseed."

When he heard about it, Favre just smiled.

"He's right," he said.

Against the Browns, Favre passed for 210 yards and three scores, and, incredibly, even ran for a touchdown.

"The guy is incredible," Rison said afterward.

But even with everything Favre was dealing with and the fact that he had matured as a quarterback, he was still a gunslinger at heart.

In a win over the Bengals later in the season, Favre drew gasps from everyone when he whistled a touchdown pass to Mark Ingram between three Bengals defenders.

Asked about the throw in the postgame press conference, Favre again smiled.

"I saw the coverage but I thought I could force it in." Suddenly Favre stopped. "No, not force, I did-n't force it. Forget that."

The room erupted in laughter. Of course, Favre still forced passes into coverage. He still threw passes from his knees and from odd angles. That's who he was and always would be. For all that he had learned, even Holmgren knew he couldn't take everything out of his quarterback.

The Packers wrapped up a playoff berth in New Orleans and could win their first division title since 1972 with a win over the Steelers in the season finale.

That provided yet another moment.

In a rugged battle on a windy, overcast day at Lambeau Field, two of the NFL's better teams slugged it out. In the fourth quarter, Favre was crushed by two Steelers defenders as he tried to get into the end zone. A staggered Favre got up slowly, clutching two trainers for support. He wobbled to the sideline, and that's when the trainers told Holmgren that Favre was spitting up blood.

Holmgren, in typical coaching fashion, asked, "How much?" Holmgren later apologized for sounding so heartless, but he knew two things: that Favre was as tough a player as he'd ever been around, and that the Packers needed him on the field.

After taking a play off, Favre returned and threw a touchdown pass. For the game, Favre was remarkable again, throwing for 301 yards and two touchdowns. It was his seventh 300-yard passing game of the season. The Packers held on for the win and the division title. It was another positive step forward. More were to come.

In the first round of the playoffs, he threw three more touchdown passes in beating the Falcons. That set up a second-round game in San Francisco against the defending Super Bowl–champion 49ers.

(opposite) Favre had a special bond with Steve Mariucci and their friendship would continue after Mariucci left to coach in San Francisco.

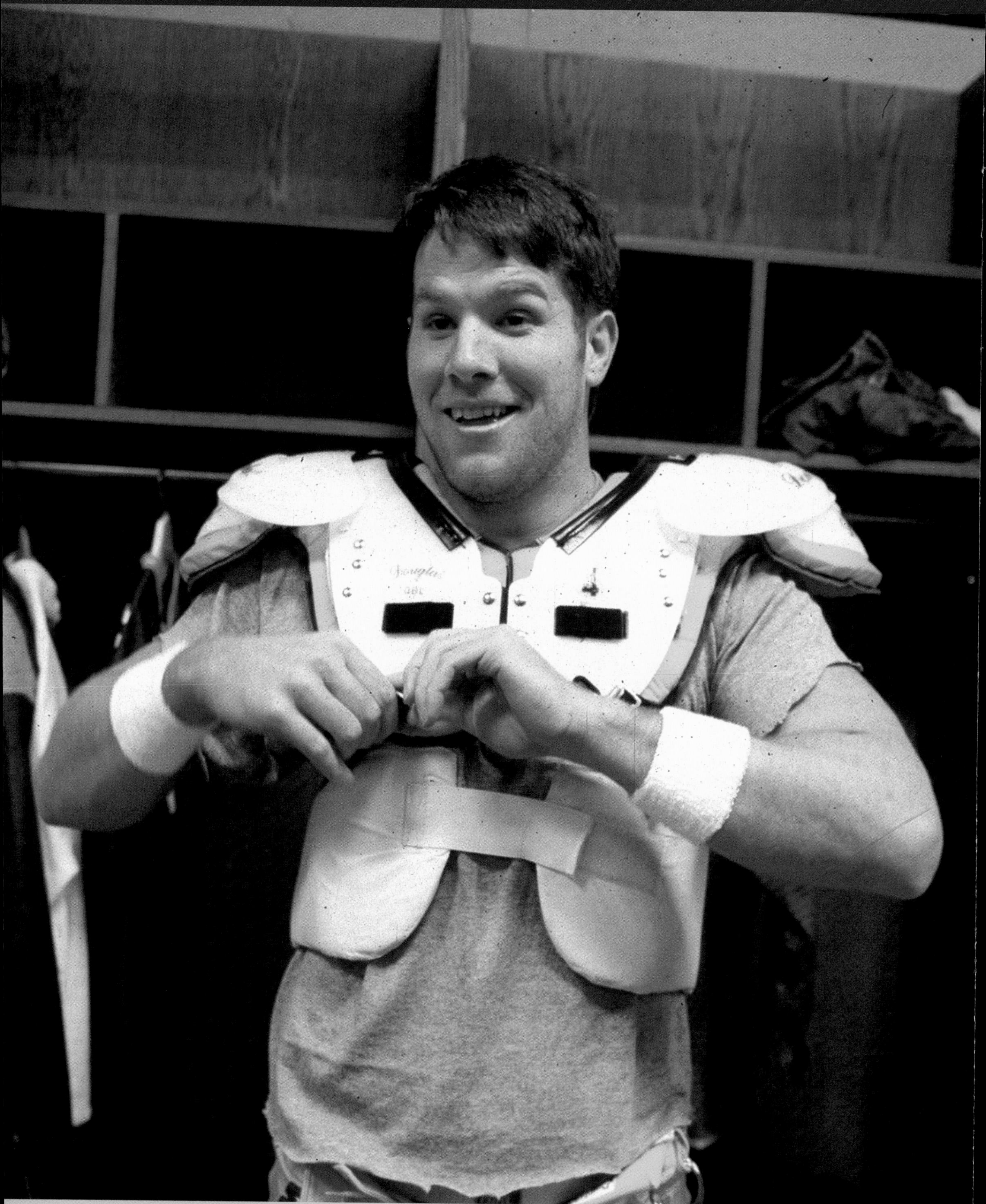

The Packers had reached the playoffs the past three seasons but had never gotten past the second round. This was another chance for this franchise to prove it really had made the strides it thought it had.

In as close to a perfect game as the Packers had ever played under Holmgren, Green Bay dominated the 'Niners. Favre was controlled and patient, completing 21 of 28 passes for 299 yards and two big first-half touchdowns. The Packers shocked the 49ers 27–17 and made yet another statement that a changing of the guard was at hand in the NFC.

Now came the Cowboys. Again.

In both 1993 and 1994, the Packers had gone to Texas Stadium and been schooled by the more experienced Cowboys. On top of that, the Packers had gone to Dallas for two regular season games and had lost those, too.

But this time—in the NFC title game—was the first time the Packers believed they belonged on the same field with the Cowboys. And for 45 minutes, the Packers carried the battle and led after three quarters.

But a costly fourth-quarter Favre interception gave the Cowboys new hope, and they went on to score two fourth-quarter touchdowns and win 38–27.

Favre was terrific in that game, throwing for 307 yards and three scores. But it wasn't enough. And as Favre and his teammates watched the Cowboys celebrate, they all silently swore they wouldn't put themselves in that position again.

It was a season for the ages for Favre. He completed 63 percent of his passes for 4,413 yards and 38 touchdowns. Amazingly, in 570 passing attempts, he only threw 13 interceptions. For that performance, he earned his first NFL Most Valuable Player.

"But it's not enough," he said afterward.

On the flight back from Dallas, Holmgren roamed the aisles and offered his demoralized troops a pep talk and a promise.

"Remember how this feels," he told them. "Don't ever forget it. We didn't get it done this time, but we will."

Indeed, from the time the plane landed, the intensity was already focused on 1996. If it was going to happen, that would be the year.

With all that anticipation and excitement, Favre's devastating announcement in May regarding his Vicodin addiction could not have shaken a community, and a team, more.

But the Packers handled the circus well. They addressed it early and quickly and then moved on—as per Holmgren's order. Nothing was going to stop this team from what everyone thought was its destiny.

Favre proved that in the impressive season-opening win over Tampa Bay. And Favre wouldn't slow down. In the first six games, in which the Packers won five, Favre threw 20 touchdown passes and just four interceptions.

Even when Favre lost his top two receivers—Robert Brooks and Antonio Freeman—and tight end Mark Chmura to injuries, the Packers kept rolling.

If anything, Favre was better in 1996 than he was in that watershed season of '95. Despite the fact that every team knew he was what made the team go and defenses were geared to slow him down, few teams were able to do it.

There was a midseason bump in the road, though, when injuries finally slowed the Packers down. The offense was decimated, and though Favre continued to play well, he simply didn't have the weapons he

(opposite) In 1995, Favre completed 63 percent of his passes for 4,413 yards and 38 touchdowns while tossing only 13 interceptions. For that performance, he earned his first NFL MVP award.

needed. The Packers went to Kansas City and lost to the Chiefs, despite a fierce Favre fourth-quarter rally. Then they went to Dallas on Monday night and held the Cowboys without a touchdown. But Dallas did kick seven field goals, and Favre was held to 194 passing yards and a last-minute touchdown in a 21–6 loss.

Suddenly, a season that seemed charmed was in danger of slipping out of control. The Packers had to go back on the road the next week to face the St. Louis Rams in another dome. By this point in Favre's career, he'd already developed a reputation as a player who struggled in domes. He was usually abysmal in the Metrodome and the Silverdome. Sure, he'd won in '96 at the Kingdome in Seattle, but now the Packers were vulnerable.

"We can't lose a third straight game," said defensive end Sean Jones. "That would signal to everyone we're in trouble."

The main concern was the offense, which had lost its earlier continuity due to injuries. In a move that smacked of near desperation, the Packers signed Andre Rison, who had worn out his welcome in Cleveland and had been released two weeks earlier by Jacksonville. But he was a veteran, was smart, was looking for a new opportunity.

Ironically, the guy who embraced him first was Favre—the guy who a year earlier had been labeled a "hayseed" by Rison.

"I've been welcomed," said Rison. "And that makes my job easier."

And he was thrown into the fire that first week in St. Louis. Favre made a point of getting him involved in the offense quickly and he did. Rison's numbers weren't anything special—five catches for 44 yards—but that was hardly the point. He was Green Bay's leading receiver, and that sent a message that the Packers would do whatever they needed to do to get the job done.

The Packers fell behind the Rams 9–0 but eventually rallied for a 24–9 victory. Favre's numbers were nothing special, either—he threw for 192 yards with two touchdowns and two interceptions. But in a game the Packers needed at a time when they weren't playing well, they had survived.

It was the turning point of the season.

Antonio Freeman, who was quickly developing into Favre's favorite receiver, returned from a broken arm the following week, and the Packers took off. They went on to win their final five games with relative ease, and Favre averaged 238 yards along with nine touchdowns and three interceptions in the four games after the win at St. Louis. The Packers rolled to a 13–3 record and the top seed in the NFC playoffs.

It was also another epic regular season for the Packers quarterback. He threw for 3,899 yards and a career-best 39 touchdowns, against just 13 interceptions. He was named the NFC's Pro Bowl quarterback and earned his second straight NFL MVP honor.

And while that was all well and good, it was not enough. He had been there and done that. He had taken the Packers to the playoffs before. Indeed, he had taken them to the brink of the Super Bowl in 1995, losing to the Cowboys.

This was it. Put up or shut up. The Packers had everything they were looking for, most especially home-field advantage in a place where it truly was a home-field advantage.

The Packers had made Lambeau Field their fortress

(opposite) Nothing was going to stop the 1996 team from what they believed was their destiny—a Super Bowl.

under Holmgren. Since a season-opening loss to the Rams in 1995, the Packers had won 16 straight there (including the playoffs). Lambeau Field had become a force, a place the players openly said was worth at least a touchdown for them.

Now there were no excuses.

The Packers earned a valuable first-round bye and used the time to heal up. Meanwhile, they awaited the winner of the 49ers-Eagles playoff battle, both of whom the Packers had already beaten that season.

The 49ers survived and relished a chance to hand the Packers an upset home loss the way Green Bay had done to the 'Niners the previous year.

And the 49ers, a force for the previous 15 years under Bill Walsh and now George Seifert, were unimpressed with what the Packers had accomplished.

"Everybody's ready to hand the Super Bowl to the Packers," 49ers tight end Brent Jones said. "They haven't won anything yet."

Favre knew this as well as anyone. He knew that until the Packers won it all, he would be just another quarterback who piled up big numbers but couldn't come through when it mattered most. He was intent to make sure that didn't happen.

On a horrid January 4 afternoon in a driving rainstorm and cold temperatures, the Packers got their chance. Directed by Holmgren to do nothing stupid and let the defense and the running game do its job, Favre obliged.

He threw only 15 passes, completed 11, and heaved one touchdown—to Andre Rison. The Packers' running game, behind Edgar Bennett, the defense, and the special teams, led by Desmond Howard, did most of the damage in a 35–14 win.

The Packers returned to the NFC title game and, this time, had it in their venue. And while Packers fans (and probably a few players) longed to get the Dallas Cowboys up to Wisconsin for a change, it wasn't to be. The upstart Carolina Panthers, behind a young quarterback named Kerry Collins and a terrific defense, had shocked the Cowboys the week before.

So the Packers would host the Panthers, and that was fine with Favre.

"These guys can play," Favre said.

Perhaps, but when they arrived at Lambeau Field, the temperature was 3 degrees, and the windchill, that lovely windchill, was 17 below zero. It was perfect Packers weather.

Favre, who hated the weather as much as the Panthers, was nervous early and made several uncharacteristic mistakes. He threw a bad interception deep in Green Bay territory that led to a Carolina touchdown.

As Favre left the field after the pick, he was taunted by Panthers linebacker Lamar Lathon.

"It's going to be a long day if you keep doing that," he said.

In the second quarter, as Favre scrambled, he fumbled, and the Panthers recovered. It led to a Carolina field goal.

"I just dropped it," Favre said later. "I thought I was done with those kinds of plays but, apparently, I'm not."

But he also vowed at that point that the stupidity was done. Play like a champ, he told himself.

Green Bay finally found its footing and, after trailing 10–7, overwhelmed the Panthers, who were simply trying to keep it close at the end. Green Bay rolled to the 30–13 win and a spot in the Super Bowl for the first time in 29 years.

(opposite) The frozen tundra of Lambeau Field was a tough place for opposing teams to play during the Packers Super Bowl seasons.

"I don't think it's really sunk in yet and I've been thinking about this all week," said Favre, who completed 19 of 29 passes for 292 yards and two touchdowns.

He was going to play in a Super Bowl for the first time, and amazingly, it would be played in the New Orleans Superdome, barely an hour from his hometown.

It was a typical two-week period prior to the Super Bowl, and Holmgren did all he could to make the time as normal as possible. But even he knew that wasn't going to happen.

The Packers were ushered off to New Orleans by a huge crowd at Lambeau Field, and once they arrived, they were easily the best story of the week.

They would play the New England Patriots, coached by the irascible genius Bill Parcells. Most pundits gave the Patriots the edge because of Parcells, but as the Packers watched more and more film of the Pats, their confidence grew.

They were so confident, in fact, that Holmgren had to force linebacker Wayne Simmons to keep his mouth shut all week.

"We're going to kill these guys," Simmons said at the time.

Favre was buffeted all week by questions about his background, his career in Green Bay, his relationship with Holmgren, his disaster in Atlanta, and playing so close to his hometown.

Favre reveled in it all. This was the stage he was waiting for, and he was going to eat it up.

But, eventually, it was time to play, and on the biggest stage in sports, Favre was equal to the challenge.

The hype was done and the interviews were fin-ished. But Favre had one final card to play. After the final practice Saturday, Holmgren gathered the entire team together and, according to one player, laid $100,000 out on a table—the amount each individual player would earn from winning the Super Bowl.

"For those of you moved by money, this is what you're playing for," Holmgren said.

He covered a lot of other topics, too, but mostly he talked about pride and finishing the job they had started so many months before.

On game day, Favre was as nervous as he had ever been before a game. It was an odd sensation. He didn't doubt his ability or the game plan. But he had an unsettled feeling that was foreign to him. Perhaps that was the first time he realized just how important this moment was.

But whatever butterflies were circling in his stomach, they disappeared quickly enough. It was Green Bay's second play from scrimmage at the Packers' 46, and Holmgren, as part of his 15 scripted plays to begin a game, had called a square-out pass to tight end Keith Jackson. But experience taught Favre to believe what he saw. He saw the Patriots' safeties playing tight man-to-man coverage, and he recognized an opportunity.

Favre audibled out of the play Holmgren had called and sent Andre Rison on a post pattern. The throw was perfect and the Packers were off and running. After the touchdown, Favre ripped off his helmet and roared in delight. This was why he played the game—and that was pure, unbridled joy.

It was a moment Bob Harlan will never forget.

"I was so nervous going into Super Bowl XXXI," he said. "I mean we hadn't been back there in so long. Then Brett threw that touchdown pass to

(opposite) In 1996 Favre was named the NFC's Pro Bowl starting quarterback and earned his second straight NFL MVP honor.

Andre Rison. He comes off the field like a little kid. He seemed so happy and so confident that it made me feel better, too. I thought then we were going to do it."

It wasn't easy. New England wrenched momentum away from the Packers and grabbed a 14–10 lead. But Favre responded with an 81-yard touchdown pass to Antonio Freeman, and he would score on a two-yard drive into the end zone later in the second quarter to give the Packers a 27–14 halftime lead.

When it was over, the Packers had beaten the Patriots 35–21. Favre completed 14 of 27 passes for 246 yards and two touchdown passes to go with his run. On most years, that likely would have been good enough to win the MVP. But Desmond Howard took the honors with his punt and kickoff returns. Favre could not have cared less.

The Patriots, however, believed Favre was the key to the Packers win.

"He showed why he's the MVP of the league," Patriots defensive coordinator Al Groh said. "His numbers belie what his effectiveness is. He's a play-maker and he can change the course of a game."

For Favre, the victory was sweet redemption. Through the injuries, the controversy, the uncertainty, the questions, he had met the challenges and answered the questions he never thought should have been asked in the first place.

"I don't know what else I've got to do to prove I'm a great quarterback," he said at the time. "I've done everything I can possibly do and I'm excited about that. There's nothing better than winning the Super Bowl."

But then came the inevitable question. What's the only thing better than winning a Super Bowl? How about winning two in a row?

Incredibly, that became the focus almost before the Packers had returned triumphantly to Green Bay with the Vince Lombardi Trophy.

And, almost as incredible, it seemed Ron Wolf had built an even stronger team in 1997. Wolf always felt that team was deeper, more versatile, more athletic than the '96 squad. But it's never quite the same the second time around. Maybe that's why it's so difficult for a Super Bowl champ to, in some cases, even get back to the playoffs the next year. The bar is set so high, the expectations are so lofty, that the task is nearly impossible.

It's what the Packers faced that next season. In fact, in a season-opening rout of the Bears at Lambeau Field on Monday night, the electricity just wasn't the same as the previous season. Oh, sure, the fans were excited, but the extra…something just wasn't there. It was what Holmgren had worried about.

Make no mistake, though, these Packers were still the class of the NFC, and they planned to prove it. And Favre, of course, was Favre.

He threw five touchdown passes in a wild win over the Vikings at Lambeau Field. He threw three awful interceptions in a loss to the Lions. A freak thunderstorm led to a missed field goal and a loss to the Eagles.

Fans who had grown accustomed to Favre doing everything well all the time were beginning to wonder what was happening as their quarterback failed to throw for 300 yards in a game through the first two months of the season.

But Favre was the same quarterback he'd always been in most respects. What many people didn't realize, though, is that tendinitis in his throwing elbow

(opposite) By the late 1990s, Favre had found professional success nearly unmatched in NFL history.

plagued him all season. It was so bad in training, he didn't even throw for weeks and, in fact, never played in the final preseason games.

And while it improved, he was never 100 percent all season. But Favre at 80 percent is still better than most quarterbacks.

Besides, Favre didn't need to overwhelm opponents with his arm anymore. He had a running game and receivers and a defense to take some of the pressure of him. But when he needed to uncork that arm, he could—and did.

In a wild loss to the previously winless Colts, Favre threw for a season-high 363 yards. The next week at Lambeau, he threw four touchdown passes in blasting the Cowboys.

It was another 13–3 season for the Packers, and Favre was marvelous again, throwing for 3,867 yards and 35 touchdowns. This year, he shared the NFL MVP award with Detroit Lions running back Barry Sanders. But that was still three MVPs in a row—something that had never happened before or since in the NFL.

Favre directed the Packers efficiently through the playoffs again, battling past the tough Tampa Bay Buccaneers and then going to San Francisco and knocking off the 49ers in the NFC title game.

For the second straight year, the Packers were back in the Super Bowl, this time in San Diego. But the edge wasn't there the way it had been in New Orleans.

The opponent was the Denver Broncos, and the Packers were installed as a staggering 14-point favorite. The Packers were no longer the NFL darlings. They were the top dogs and, as such, they were the ones viewed as the evil empire. It was time for someone to take them down—at least in the eyes of many NFL fans.

And, as several Packers admitted afterward, they committed the cardinal sin in pro sports—they took their opponent for granted.

It didn't appear that way in the beginning, as the Packers moved methodically down the field and scored on a Favre-to-Freeman touchdown pass.

The Packers and Broncos whacked away at each other all day, but it was the play of running back Terrell Davis that tormented the Packers' defense all day. The Packers fell behind 31–24 late in the fourth quarter when Holmgren made the controversial decision to let Davis score a touchdown with just under two minutes to play so the Packers could get the ball back.

Favre got the Packers into Denver territory in the closing seconds before a fourth-down pass over the middle intended for Mark Chmura fell incomplete.

It was over. Favre stood there, hands on his hips, unable to conceive of the fact that he had fallen short. His numbers were good—25 of 42 for 256 yards and two touchdowns. But he threw a costly interception and fumbled, as well.

"We just didn't get it done," Favre said afterward, as though he still couldn't believe it.

And he discovered what he always hoped he never would—just how badly it hurt to lose a Super Bowl.

But there would be another year. Of that, he was certain. The franchise was too good, the plan too solid, the players too committed. There would be next year. ■

(opposite) For Favre, the Super Bowl victory was sweet redemption, and he would return to the NFL championship game the following season to square off with John Elway and the Denver Broncos.

Starting Over

It is the problem inherent with being at the top of any profession. Eventually, predictably, the decline must begin. Sometimes it's fast and sometimes it takes a few years. But it always happens. It has to. It is the way of all things.

Players get older. Other teams improve. The motivation wavers. The luck changes. It happens.

For the Green Bay Packers, it seemed the joy ride had just begun when it already appeared that it was coming to an end.

The face of the Packers was already changing. General manager Ron Wolf was starting to talk about how the grind of building the team was wearing him out. Mike Holmgren had been in Green Bay six years, had taken the team to two Super Bowls, and was wondering what else might be out there. Reggie White was contemplating retirement (and would retire after the season).

Some from the Super Bowl run—like Sean Jones and Keith Jackson—had already retired. Others like Desmond Howard, Andre Rison, Doug Evans, and Don Beebe had moved on. Cornerback Craig Newsome had to quit due to a bad knee, and dependable wide receiver Robert Brooks, also with a bad knee, was trying to hang on for another season.

Brett Favre saw all his teammates melting away. His friends like Doug Pederson, Jim McMahon, Mark Brunell, and Ty Detmer were with other teams. The faces were changing and the game was changing, too.

The pieces that made the Packers the NFL gold standard for the last few years weren't there anymore.

Favre still played for the love of the game and still had the belief that the Packers were good enough to make it back to the Super Bowl. But the dynamic was shifting, and not necessarily for the better.

The biggest change Favre sensed was in his head coach. Holmgren had grown antsy. The loss in Super Bowl XXXII, and the criticism that followed, angered and confused him.

He had given everything to the Packers, and now he felt that maybe it was time to move on. He had reached a level of respect and power in the league, and he wanted what the other top-name coaches had: the title of general manager.

Bill Parcells had it. So did Mike Shanahan in Denver. Holmgren felt he was every bit the equal of those two, and others, in his ability to find talent.

He wanted the power and the prestige, and he knew he wasn't going to get it so long as Ron Wolf

(opposite) After winning a Super Bowl so early in his career, Favre seemed to be walking on air.

was still in town. In the classic analogy, Green Bay simply wasn't big enough for the two massive egos each man owned.

So those were the thoughts swirling through the air in the 1998 season.

As well, the Packers' dominance was already being challenged in the NFC in general and, most especially, in the NFC Central Division, where the Minnesota Vikings had built a powerhouse.

A great draft had landed them a young stud wide receiver, Randy Moss, and that concerned Green Bay. Randall Cunningham was a savvy veteran quarterback, and the Vikings' defense, which had tormented the Packers even when Green Bay was at the top of its game, was fast, mean, and hungry.

But those were all issues that would be dealt with in due course.

Favre put the blinders on and went into the season convinced everything was where it should and would be.

He got off to another fast start, throwing 10 touchdown passes in his first four games, including a remarkable five against the Carolina Panthers in a game they had won, then lost, and then won again.

But it was already clear that in this season everything would come down to the wire.

Then came a Monday night battle between two unbeaten teams: the Packers and the upstart Vikings. The Packers had all the confidence—after all, they owned teams at Lambeau, having won 25 in a row. But a changing of the guard, of sorts, was seen on that drizzly night.

The Vikings, behind the incredible Moss, tore up the Packers in front of a national TV audience. Favre never could get untracked and completed just 13 of 23 passes for 114 yards and three interceptions. He also didn't throw a touchdown pass for the first time in 21 games, including the playoffs.

The loss had shaken the Packers' confidence in more ways than one. Minnesota had physically dominated Green Bay. It played smarter. It played with more passion. It played like a team that had something to prove. And the Vikings went into Lambeau unafraid and hit the Packers right in the mouth.

"I didn't think we could be handled like that," a stunned Favre said afterward.

And for the rest of the season, it seemed as though the Packers were playing in the Vikings' shadow, a place no Packers player ever figured he'd be.

That loss started a downward streak for Favre. In the next four games, Favre threw a disquieting nine interceptions and just seven touchdowns. He had reverted, in some ways, back to the reckless gunslinger of his earlier career. It was a phase Holmgren, the fans, and Favre figured had been left far behind.

But through the first nine games of the season, he had already thrown 16 interceptions, more than he threw the entire season in either 1995 or 1996.

So, of course, the questions began. What was wrong with Brett Favre? Was he hurt? Was he pressing? Was he back on painkillers? Rumors ran rampant that he was being seen in downtown Appleton, a city 20 miles south of Green Bay with a vibrant nightlife. He was cruising the bars, drunk and out of control.

Favre smiled when heard the rumors.

"If I did half the stuff I was accused of doing, I'd be dead by now," he said.

The fact was, teams had begun to figure out the

Packers' offensive scheme, and the weapons he'd had in the two Super Bowls years weren't there any-more. Probably Favre was pressing as he tried to acclimate new receivers into the system but, mostly, it was the realization that every good thing must end. Or at least start anew.

But some things don't improve. And as the season wore on, more rumors pummeled the franchise. Holmgren was clearly unhappy now, and some peo-ple began to think his attitude was affecting the team's performance.

That situation reached a stunning nadir in a November 29 home game against the lowly Eagles. The Packers had played a poor first half against an already struggling team playing with a third-team quarterback.

Leading by just a field goal at the break, Holmgren was walking off the field to the locker room when one fan told the coach to concentrate on where he was and not where he was going. Holmgren erupted and stalked toward the stands and the fan before security personnel had to restrain him.

It was a shocking development. Mike Holmgren was practically a god in Wisconsin. He could do no wrong in the eyes of just about everyone. He had made Green Bay his home and he had given back to the community time and again. Winning a Super Bowl had given him carte blanche, but it had also raised the expectations for the team to nearly impossible levels.

Perhaps it was just a culmination of the frustra-tion of a season that wasn't going as hoped, or maybe that fan touched a nerve. Maybe Holmgren was distracted. Whatever it was, it signaled that the Holmgren era was coming to a close.

The Packers regrouped and so did Favre.

After 16 interceptions in the first nine games, he threw just seven in the final seven and added 14 touchdown passes.

Indeed, despite a turbulent regular season, Favre had posted more eye-popping numbers. He led the NFL in passing yards with 4,212 and completions with 347. He was also third in the NFC, with 31 touchdown passes.

And while his streak of three straight NFL Most Valuable Player awards was snapped, it was obvious to everyone that this was a quarterback at the top of his game and the peak of his ability. And as long as Favre was behind center, that made the Packers a very dangerous team.

Again, the power had shifted in the NFC. Whereas, Green Bay, San Francisco, and Dallas had dominated the conference the previous few years, this season the Vikings and Atlanta Falcons were the flavor of the moment.

But like two old fighters who still had plenty up their sleeves, the Packers and 'Niners reached the playoffs on guile, experience, and just enough talent.

And in as attractive a wild-card playoff game as football fans could hope for, the 49ers, behind Steve Young, would host the Packers, with Brett Favre.

And the back stories were even better.

Favre's long-time friend, Steve Mariucci, was coaching the 49ers, and Holmgren, a San Francisco native and former 'Niners assistant coach, longed to one day to return the franchise and the city he loved so much.

There were more rumors: this time that if Mariucci, who had been beaten three times by his

(opposite) In 1998 Favre got off to another fast start, throwing 10 touchdown passes in his first four games.

mentor Holmgren, lost this playoff game, he would be fired. Holmgren's name was being attached to every opening, real or imagined, in the NFL.

It got so bad that it was believed that if the Packers won again, Holmgren would in fact replace Mariucci with the 49ers, and Mariucci, a Packers fan as a kid growing up in the Upper Peninsula of Michigan, would take Holmgren's spot in Green Bay.

On one level, it made sense. But on all the others, it didn't. For one thing, Holmgren wanted to be a general manager and coach, and the 49ers had just hired a new GM. Second, Wolf would never have hired Mariucci in Green Bay because he didn't embody what Wolf wanted in a head coach. He wanted a tough guy with players, not a buddy.

So it was more than a game when the two old warriors met at Candlestick Park. And if it was to be Holmgren's last game with the Packers, he would go out having been part of classic.

Favre and Young were brilliant, and the two teams whacked away at each other all afternoon, with momentum shifting at least four times. The Packers led 17–10 at halftime thanks mostly to a great running game provided by veteran Dorsey Levens. But the 49ers seemed to take control of the game for good in the fourth quarter, grabbing a 23–20 lead and then intercepting Favre with five minutes to play.

But the Packers got the ball back, and Favre hit Corey Bradford on a bomb that put the Packers in position to take the lead. With just under two minutes left, Favre did what he does best. He audibled out of Holmgren's play call, a sweep, and into a play he had run only once before with wide receiver Antonio Freeman. Freeman shook his defender and caught Favre's perfect pass for what appeared to be

the game-winning TD and another dagger in the 49ers' heart.

But this was a different season. The previous three years, it's likely that would have been it. But not this season and not with Steve Young.

Aided by a questionable non-fumble call on wide receiver Jerry Rice, the 49ers roared back downfield and, with three seconds left, Young hit Terrell Owens over the middle and between three Packers defenders for the touchdown.

It was a stunning and unbelievable conclusion to a season that really had felt precarious right from the beginning.

Ron Wolf fumed after the game about the non-fumble.

"The team with the most points won that game," he said.

Favre, who completed 20 of 35 passes for 292 yards and two scores, tried to shrug it off.

"We can sit here all day and make excuses," he said. "It was one of those great ballgames."

The 49ers would end up losing to the Falcons the following week, and the Falcons shocked the once-beaten Vikings in the NFC title game. But no one in Green Bay really cared. For the first time since 1994, the Packers weren't a major player in the play-offs, and it felt surreal, foreign.

And more was to come.

In Holmgren's postseason press conference he refused to say whether his days in Green Bay were done. Events had moved to warp speed, but no one really knew what was happening.

Then the answers started coming. Mariucci was given a contract extension to stay in San Francisco and, five days after losing to the 'Niners, Holmgren

(opposite) Mike Holmgren led the Packers to the top of the football world, but soon he too would be off to new challenges.

was named the general manager and head coach of the Seattle Seahawks.

And while it wasn't really a surprise to anyone who had been keeping tabs on the developing soap opera, it was still something no one could fathom. Holmgren had been with the Packers for seven years, but it had seemed like a lifetime.

In that time, he had taken a forlorn franchise and turned it into the game's best. And he had brought the state of Wisconsin along with it. There had been five straight playoff appearances, two trips to the Super Bowl, and one championship. It's more than most franchises could hope for—and to happen in a little place like Green Bay made it even more amazing.

But now it was time to move on. Favre never really spoke publicly about Holmgren's departure. It happened right after the season ended, so Favre was already back in Mississippi. He was out of communication, clearly the way the Packers wanted it.

Some players were convinced it was time for the relationship to move on. Favre and Holmgren still got along, and both men still respected what each had to say, but Favre had learned just about everything he was going to learn from his head coach. And there comes a time in every sport, no matter the level, where players begin to tune out what the coach is saying. It's just the way of sports. And it reached that stage in Green Bay.

Holmgren related several years later that he would have stayed in Green Bay (he had just built a new home there) if he had received any indication that he might get a chance to be the general manager. But Wolf, though he was thinking about stepping away, was not at that stage yet.

Ironically, Wolf walked away two years later, and Bob Harlan would impart the same GM/head coach duties on Mike Sherman that Holmgren had always coveted.

But in early 1999 Wolf was still in charge and he wanted to move quickly to fill Holmgren's immense void. He wanted a tough guy, a coach who would instill fear and respect, and his focus fell on one man and one man only—Ray Rhodes.

Rhodes had been defensive coordinator for the Packers in Holmgren's first two years but left suddenly citing his and his family's uncomfortable feelings in Green Bay. Now, however, Rhodes was available after just being released as coach of the Eagles.

"I thought Ray was everything we were looking for," Wolf said.

So certain was he that he didn't interview anyone else for the job. He didn't even consider Packers long-time offensive coordinator Sherm Lewis, who desperately wanted a chance to be a head coach.

Wolf knew what he wanted and he wanted Rhodes. The humorless Rhodes, the complete opposite of Holmgren, quickly accepted the job and announced immediately he had no intention of fixing something that wasn't broken.

If Favre was concerned, he didn't say anything about it. He was pleased that Lewis would be retained as offensive coordinator, but he'd be working with a new quarterbacks coach, a young guy by the name of Mike McCarthy. Favre and McCarthy forged a strong relationship that continued seven years later when McCarthy was named Packers head coach.

Rhodes's first, and only, season in Green Bay got off to a rocky start when Favre suffered a severe

(opposite) It was obvious to everyone that Favre was a quarterback at the top of his game and the peak of his ability.

thumb injury in a preseason win over Denver. He gutted his way through the season, but it never healed properly.

The Packers opened the Rhodes era with a come-from-behind win over the Raiders that saw Favre break down in tears afterward. He threw for 333 yards and four touchdowns, but he also threw three interceptions. And it became clear that the Packers had hit a rough patch as they tried to move forward.

The bottom might have been hit in an October 17 game in Denver when the Packers barely showed up. They were routed by the Broncos 31–10, and Favre was awful. He completed just seven of 23 passes for 120 yards and he was picked off three times. Favre drew criticism after the game when he was seen laughing and cracking jokes with Denver players as the spanking was going on.

But Favre did take the loss, and the direction, seriously. On the plane trip back from Denver, Favre sat with Rhodes and expressed his concern about where this franchise was going. Rhodes nodded and said little.

It only got worse two weeks later when, on a Monday night in Green Bay against his old coach, the Packers were clobbered by the Seahawks 27–7. In that game Favre completed just 14 of 35 passes for 180 yards. He threw one touchdown but four interceptions.

In a suddenly interminable season, there were still highlights. Perhaps the best came in November against Chicago when Favre started his 117th consecutive game, breaking the all-time quarterback durability record held by Ron Jaworski. It's a mark that continues today.

Favre probably saved his best game for last as he threw for 311 yards and two scores for a win over the Cardinals. That got the Packers to 8–8, but they missed the playoffs for the first time since 1993.

Favre's numbers dropped perceptibly that season. Though he threw for 4,091 yards, his completion percentage dropped to 57 percent, and he had just 22 touchdown passes and 23 interceptions.

Wolf had already seen enough. By midseason, he thought he might have made a mistake hiring Rhodes. By the end of the season, he was sure of it.

The team was undisciplined, it practiced poorly, it had no fire. It reminded Wolf of 1991, the year he took over the team. And he was going to stop it before it got any worse.

So the evening after the season finale, Wolf fired Rhodes. And this time he took his time finding a replacement. He interviewed, almost as a courtesy, a former Packers tight ends coach named Mike Sherman, who was then offensive coordinator/tight ends coach in Seattle with Holmgren. Wolf was so impressed with Sherman and his vision for the franchise that he stunned everyone by hiring him, even though he had interviewed more high-profile coaches like Marty Schottenheimer.

Sherman, again, was different from Holmgren but was more in the mold of what seemed to work for the franchise.

Again Favre took the changes in stride, decided it wouldn't really change how he played, and he plowed ahead. And every season, he would say the same thing: This team can win. This team has talent.

And he would say that as long as he was having fun, he would continue to play. But even Favre admitted it wasn't as much fun as it used to be. ■

(opposite) Despite the team's ups and downs, Favre always believed the Packers could win games.

A Question of Playing

Brett Favre could hardly remember a time when he wasn't playing football. It was all he knew. And it was everything that he loved.

But for the first time, as he approached the age when many NFL quarterbacks begin to question their mortality, Favre began to wonder how much was left in the tank.

It was a new century, a new team, and in some respects, a new game. The players he had started with continued to fade away and, at age 31, Favre was looking at what else might be down the road for him. Mike Holmgren had been gone only two years, but it might as well have been 22 with all the changes that had occurred in the franchise since his departure.

Ray Rhodes had come and gone as head coach and had taken much of the Packers' soul with him. An 8–8 record in 1999 was the team's worst in eight years, and missing the playoffs was a shock to the system for players and fans alike. That performance cost Rhodes his job after just one season, a move that stunned even Rhodes's detractors.

After all, it had only been one season, and no one can judge anything in one year, can they?

Wolf felt he could, especially after he saw how the team enthusiasm and discipline had disintegrated as the year went on.

And yet, with that all that, the Packers were within an eyelash of returning to the playoffs. Even more telling was Wolf's insistence, then and now, that if the Packers had made the playoffs that year, he would have fired Rhodes. It was the kind of indictment rarely seen in sports.

Everyone was starting over. Rhodes was out and in was the dour Mike Sherman, who had never been a head coach at any level anywhere. But Wolf loved Sherman's attention to detail and his realization of just how important the Packers' mystique was.

As for Favre, his game really hadn't tailed off. He still threw for more than 4,000 yards in 1999, but he didn't have as much to show for it. And there would be more changes. Favre had started with Steve Mariucci as his quarterbacks coach. Then came Andy Reid, followed by Marty Mornhinweg, and then Mike McCarthy. When Rhodes was fired, so were all the assistants, and now Favre had to learn all over again.

Sherman was schooled at the knee of Mike Holmgren, and that included calling his own plays. He did hire Tom Rossley as offensive coordinator

(opposite) In 2000, Favre began to wonder for the first time how much was left in his tank.

and quarterbacks coach, but, as in the Holmgren years, the head coach called the plays.

Favre always had a knack for adapting to the situation. If it was a new scheme, a new wrinkle, a new coach, he would do whatever needed to be done. He may not have always liked it, and as the years went on he began voicing his opinions more openly, but he always followed the plan.

Sherman and Rossley recognized that Favre may not be the quarterback he was five years earlier and that restraint might need to make its way into Favre's game. He didn't agree, but he'd do what he was asked.

In 2000 the Packers again missed the playoffs with a 9–7 record, despite closing with four straight wins. Favre threw for a respectable 3,812 yards, but his 20 touchdown passes were his fewest since 1993. His 16 interceptions were also his fewest since 1997.

Many felt Favre, and the Packers, were at the proverbial crossroads. Here was one of the dominant teams in the 1990s and it had missed the playoffs two years in a row.

Favre's consecutive-games streak continued

(opposite) The players he broke into the league with were now retiring and at age 31, Favre started looking at what might be down the road for him. (above) Favre has been the unquestioned leader of the Packers throughout his career.

unabated, but at what cost? Was he still the Packers' best quarterback or was he playing just to be playing?

The Packers drafted quarterback upon quarterback over the years, but none got a shot because of Favre's remarkable durability. Ty Detmer. Mark Brunell. T.J. Rubley. Jim McMahon. Doug Pederson. Steve Bono. Danny Wuerffel. Craig Nall. Ronnie McAda. Aaron Brooks. Matt Hasselbeck. So many others. And still Favre endured.

As the questions were being asked, another bombshell fell. A month after the 2000 season ended, Ron Wolf decided it was time to retire. Another cog in that formidable machine was gone. Wolf, the guy who had gambled everything on an unknown number-three quarterback in Atlanta, was finally done.

"I'll never be able to say what Ron Wolf means to me," Favre said.

But everyone knew. He gave the kid a chance, and the kid didn't disappoint.

Team president Bob Harlan moved quickly and, in a surprise, gave Sherman the dual titles of general manager and head coach—exactly what Holmgren had sought so desperately two years earlier.

But just when it seemed the Packers were on the slow slide back into mediocrity, something remarkable happened. Bolstered by a rejuvenated running game led by Ahman Green and the still youthful Favre, the Packers roared back to life in 2001.

The Packers posted an impressive 12–4 record, and Favre was one of the main reasons. He was back. He threw for 3,921 yards and 32 touchdowns, his highest total since 1997.

It was like the mid-'90s again, and the Packers were doing what NFL teams weren't supposed to be able to do anymore—reload and flourish in the days of free agency. But the story was always the same: as long as the Packers had Brett Favre, they had a chance to be successful.

Yet there were always those two sides of Brett Favre. He could manufacture plays out of nothing. He could make throws no one else could make. He was what made the Packers go every game. And when he didn't, the Packers suffered.

And in a playoff game against the young, strong, confident St. Louis Rams, everything that could go wrong did.

The Rams, who would go on to win the Super Bowl that season, warmed up by crushing Green Bay 45–17, the worst loss in the Packers' proud playoff history.

Favre was 26 of 44 for 281 yards. Not bad. But then there were the six interceptions he threw up to the grateful Rams defense. Worse, three of those picks were returned for touchdowns, and a fourth set up another touchdown.

It was Brett Favre at his worst, and as fans and opponents had come to learn, a bad Brett Favre was absolutely toxic.

"The one thing you don't want to do in any game is have turnovers," Favre said afterward in a study of understatement.

To Favre's credit, over the years he has rarely ducked the postgame autopsies. There have only been a handful of games in his career when he begged off talking about bad performances or tough losses. And he faced the music after this disaster. But this was the first year when the talk really began as to how much longer Favre figured he

(opposite) The Packers drafted quarterback upon quarterback over the years but none got a shot because of Favre's remarkable durability.

might play. And his answer was always the same.

In 2002 the Packers perhaps came the closest to seeing what life without Favre would be like. In an October 20 game against the Washington Redskins, Favre started for the 164th straight time. But he didn't finish.

As he was being sacked by Redskins linebacker LaVar Arrington, Favre's left knee twisted awkwardly and painfully. Packers fans had grown accustomed to seeing him pop up from such tackles, but this time he didn't.

"My stomach dropped," coach Mike Sherman said at the time.

He was eventually helped off the field in a tomb-silent Lambeau Field, and numerous doctors hovered over him, diagnosing his injury. Then he was taken to the locker room on the infamous golf cart, his head covered by a towel.

"I thought I was done for the year," Favre said later. "That's the first time I ever felt that way."

As it turned out, Favre suffered a sprained lateral collateral ligament—not disastrous, but bad enough. In fact, if the Packers had to play the next week, Favre's streak likely would have ended. But luck was on their side as Green Bay had a bye week, allowing him to heal enough to play the next game against Miami.

And play he did. Wearing a bulky knee brace for the first time in his career, Favre played carefully and intelligently, completing 16 of 25 passes for 187 yards in the 24–10 win.

Favre's résumé had another addition to it.

Despite that injury, it was another terrific season for Favre and for the Packers, who stormed to another 12–4 record. Favre completed 341 of 551 passes for 3,658 yards with 27 touchdowns and just 16 interceptions. He was named player of the year by *Sports Illustrated* and fell four votes short of winning a fourth NFL MVP award.

But, for the second straight year, postseason frustration shattered what had been a great regular. This time, the upstart Atlanta Falcons came to Lambeau Field, where the Packers had never lost a playoff game, and dominated Green Bay 27–7. It was the Packers' first home playoff loss in 13 games, dating back to 1939.

It was a subpar effort on just about everybody's part, including Favre, who looked lethargic and a step slow. The Falcons rolled to a 24–0 halftime lead, and the Packers never showed any signs of rallying. Favre did throw for 247 yards, but he was also intercepted twice.

The Packers had won 24 games the previous two years and had nothing to show for it. The frustration was beginning to grow as the 2003 season dawned.

Favre wasn't getting any younger, and that infamous window that teams have to win a championship was already starting to close again. Favre no doubt saw it, sensed it, but had no intention of going down without a fight. And 2003 is no better example of that.

For the second straight year, Favre found himself in a position where his unbelievable playing streak could end. In an October 19 loss to St. Louis Favre broke his right thumb when his hand hit the helmet of teammate Mike Wahle.

As was the case the previous year, Favre's serious injury was followed by a week off, allowing a chance for recovery. But this was the thumb of his throwing hand. He couldn't really grip the ball, and

(opposite) Although questions persisted about diminishing skills as he got older, Favre's leadership capabilities have never been doubted.

it hurt when he tried to do anything.

Pain aside, the Packers faced a crucial game against the Minnesota Vikings in the Metrodome, and Favre was determined to play.

"I was telling myself most of the time, 'You're stupid. Of all the times you could actually back out of a game and no one would question it, this is it,'" he said. "But I really wanted to play and redeem myself, broken thumb or not."

Favre did indeed play, again managing the game superbly and throwing for 194 yards and two touchdowns in a 30–27 win.

But that was nothing compared to what would occur December 22. In the game that more than any other may end up defining Favre as a person and player, he took the field in Oakland on a Monday night. Just hours earlier, he had been told on a Bay Area golf course that his beloved dad, Irvin, had suffered a heart attack and died back in Mississippi. Favre was determined to play in the game, though he admitted later, he wasn't even sure where he was or what he was doing.

"But I couldn't let everyone down," he said.

He was nervous in warm-ups and couldn't remember the last time he'd been nervous warming up for a game. And then everything came into focus. The game slowed down and Brett Favre was back in the zone his dad had always taught him to find.

In front of a sympathetic national audience, Favre was simply spectacular. He threw for 399 yards and four touchdowns as the Packers routed the Raiders 41–7.

When it was over, every teammate and nearly every Raider hugged him. That's respect. It is what a player of his caliber has earned after years of play-ing the game the way it needed to be played.

In a season of emotional turmoil, the Packers posted a 10–6 record, Favre fired another 32 touchdown passes, and Green Bay was back in the playoffs thanks to a last-minute loss by the Vikings in Arizona that the amazed Packers watched with their enthralled fans at Lambeau.

And the emotions weren't done yet. The Packers won their playoff opener in overtime when cornerback Al Harris returned an interception for a touchdown against the Seattle Seahawks and Mike Holmgren.

That set up a second-round game in Philadelphia against the Eagles—a game Packers fans still think about in amazement.

The Packers outplayed the Eagles most of the game and seemed to have it wrapped up as the Eagles faced fourth down and 26. Incredibly, quarterback Donovan McNabb hit Freddie Mitchell for 28 yards and the first down. Soon after, David Akers kicked a field goal with two seconds remaining to tie the game and send it to overtime.

In overtime, Favre launched a pass toward Javon Walker that was intercepted and returned 35 yards by Brian Dawkins. Akers kicked another field goal, and that was that.

It was an unbelievable conclusion to a turbulent season—the Packers had been this close to returning to the NFC title game.

There were repercussions for that late-game collapse. Sherman fired both Tom Rossley and defensive coordinator Ed Donatell, moves many thought far too rash.

The 2004 season saw Favre throw for another 4,000 yards and 30 touchdowns, but there were

(opposite) Favre walks off the field with his wife, Deanna, following a heroic performance in his first game after his father died.

more injuries. He suffered a concussion in a game against the New York Giants but stayed in long enough to throw a touchdown pass he still doesn't remember.

The Packers won 10 more games, but another first-round playoff exit followed, this time authored by the Minnesota Vikings.

The personal numbers were piling up for Favre, but they weren't leading to anything. Even he began to wonder just how much longer it made sense to play. There were more injuries and they were taking longer and longer to recover from. Was it worth it? His two daughters were growing up and his wife had survived a battle with breast cancer. His priorities were changing, and he could feel it. But still the game pulled at him, and he was encouraged by his family to keep playing if that's what he wanted.

And, despite everything, he still wanted to play and he still felt he could make a difference. ■

(opposite) Favre always shared a close relationship with his father, Irv. (above) In 2002, Favre was named player of the year by *Sports Illustrated* and fell four votes short of winning a fourth NFL MVP award.

Rejuvenation

Brett Favre had been through everything in his 13 years with the Green Bay Packers. He had watched the franchise struggle, grow up, flourish, decline, and blossom again. It had, frankly, been one of a hell of a ride and one he wouldn't have missed for the world.

But what's the phrase? That which doesn't kill us makes us stronger? That was Favre's career with the Packers for nearly two years.

He had suffered through some the worst injuries and emotional turmoil of his career. And through some mystical combination of karma, blind luck, toughness, and guile, he continued to play though it all. But that determination to play wasn't paying the dividends it once had.

The Packers kept winning in the regular season but, for whatever reason, that success wasn't translating to the postseason. Indeed, Favre had played some the worst football of his career in the recent postseason.

It was unavoidable now. Favre had to deal with the question of how much longer he would play. Everyone was asking, and he really didn't have an answer.

He always swore he wouldn't be one of those pathetic caricatures who kept playing long after they were effective. He still loved football and the competition. But training camp had grown intolerable. Practices were torture. Film work a study is masochism.

What still made it worthwhile were the games. There was no substitute for that. It was like a drug, an addiction, and he knew the day that playing on Sundays no longer tripped his trigger, he would quit. He knew all that. But he also knew deep down he could still compete and, more to the point, he could make the Packers better.

The 2003 season had taken a lot out of him. The Packers had been so close to getting to the NFC title game and another Super Bowl. They had played so well and were very likely the best team in the NFC when it mattered most. But they couldn't close the deal against the Eagles, and "fourth and 26" had become a cruel, cursed phrase among Packers fans.

Favre took his share of criticism as well for the bizarre, poorly thrown ball that was intercepted in overtime and led to the game-winning field goal.

Changes were coming. That was clear. And one that was far from unexpected came in the April

(opposite) Favre had watched the franchise struggle, grow up, flourish, decline, and blossom again.

AP Wide-World

2005 draft when the Packers, picking 24th, saw California quarterback Aaron Rodgers fall down to them.

Uncharacteristically, the Packers jumped at the opportunity and selected the strong-armed QB. He would be Favre's successor. He would learn at the knee of the master and then move seamlessly into Favre's spot when the old pro retired.

Favre shrugged off the move and made it clear rather quickly that he had no intention of being a teacher.

"He can figure it out like everybody else," he said. "I don't have time to teach him."

As it turned out, 2005 wouldn't be a season anyone would want to learn anything from anybody in the organization, unless it was how to lose close games in agonizing fashion.

Green Bay opened the season with four straight losses, and it never got any better. Every game, it seemed, a disastrous mistake would lead to another loss. The Packers lost seven games by a total of 21 points. They were blown out only twice, but when it happened, it was awful.

In a loss at Cincinnati, Favre was intercepted a

(opposite) Favre knew deep down that he could still play at the highest level and make the Packers a better team. (above) Farve was as surprised as anyone when the Packers drafted Aaron Rodgers in 2005.

Remarkably, Favre thought he was in danger of becoming an aging hanger-on who didn't know when it was time to walk away.

mind-numbing five times. In another loss to the Chicago Bears, he was picked off four times. In fact, of the 16 games he played, he threw at least one interception in 14. And he managed just one touchdown pass in his final five games. The Packers crashed to a 4–12 record, their worst since the bad old days of Lindy Infante in 1991.

Favre still threw for 3,881 yards, but he also threw a career-high 29 interceptions, by far the most in the NFL. He was in danger of becoming what he always swore he wouldn't—an aging hanger-on who didn't know when it was time to walk away.

In the season finale, a 23–17 win over the thoroughly disinterested Seattle Seahawks, Favre acknowledged the Lambeau crowd in a way that suggested to many that he was done. Sensing something might be happening, the throng chanted, "One more year," as Favre continued to wave and smile.

After the game, coach Mike Sherman presented Favre with the game ball, and Favre broke down.

"He sure was emotional, that's for sure," backup quarterback Craig Nall said.

Favre also blew off his traditional postgame press conference, leading to even more speculation that the great quarterback had really had enough.

That led to an offseason unlike any this franchise has ever seen before.

The first shoe dropped just a few days after the season ended when Sherman was fired. Despite six seasons, including four that included the playoffs, it was clear to many in the organization that, as with Holmgren, the players had begun to tune him out.

General manager Ted Thompson, who had taken the GM duties from Sherman a few months earlier, then began an exhaustive search for his replacement. Favre, who had remained silent since walking out of Lambeau after the Seahawks game, watched intently from his Mississippi compound.

After interviewing a number of candidates, Thompson settled on San Francisco 49ers offensive coordinator Mike McCarthy who, like Sherman before, had never been a head coach anywhere. But McCarthy knew Favre and the Packers after his one season under Ray Rhodes in 1999. He was tough, hard-nosed, not especially eloquent, but devoted to football. Whether his hiring would be enough to convince Favre to return, no one knew. But this much was clear. The Packers were going to give Favre as much time as he needed to decide.

"I knew there was some unhappiness in Brett's mind with the play-calling," Packers president Bob Harlan said. "Brett came to my office one day, and we talked about it. I told him I was going to hire Ted Thompson as the general manager, and he seemed to like that. I thought it would help him make his decision."

Harlan also made it clear the Packers weren't going to push Favre for an answer until he was ready to give it.

"People would call me and ask me if I thought he was returning, and I always said, 'I think he's coming back,'" Harlan said. "He's such a competitor and as long as he can compete and he can help the team, I always thought he was going to

come back. But that's all I had to base it on because I didn't know either."

For the next four months, Favre and the Packers would dance around each other. Favre wanted assurances that the Packers would improve the offense to allow them to compete the following season. He called Thompson and McCarthy on occasion to stay in touch, but there were still no guarantees of anything.

Harlan recalled, "Ted would tell me, 'I talked to Brett today. I talked for five minutes and he talked for 45 minutes.' That's just how it was. I just wanted it over. We all wanted a positive answer to come back."

In one especially bizarre sequence over the summer, rumors circulated that Favre would announce his decision at his annual golf tournament in Mississippi.

A battalion of national media rolled into the bayou awaiting word, but an incredulous Favre said he had never said anything. The rumor was just that. He had still made no decision and he still wasn't sure when he would.

It was an embarrassing episode for Favre, who

(above) The national media descended on a charity golf event Favre was hosting, wondering if he was going to announce his retirement.

Riddell

was now beginning to look as though he was taking the patient Packers organization for a ride.

Favre also issued a quote he later regretted when he was asked if he was taking too long to decide his future.

"What are they going to do?" Favre asked. "Cut me?"

It was a flip and cavalier answer that didn't seem worthy of Favre or the situation. And Favre soon realized that all the tons of goodwill he had built up over the years was in danger of slipping away because of how this situation was being handled.

Finally in July, just prior to training camp, Favre decided he would return. He liked some of the young talent that Thompson had stockpiled and he figured it was worth at least one more season. But after being shut out by the Bears in the season-opener, Favre openly wondered what he had gotten himself into.

As the quarterback of the youngest team in the NFL, though, Favre knew it would take some time. And by the end of the season, it all began to make sense to the youngsters. The Packers won their final four games, and Favre, playing within the system McCarthy demanded, was having fun again. Green Bay finished with an 8–8 record that no one would have predicted in September. Favre threw 613 passes, the most in his career, for 3,885 yards. He only threw 18 touchdown passes, but he only had 18 interceptions, as well. Favre was playing like a kid again.

But, as was the case the previous season, the big question loomed. He closed out the season with a home win, this time over the Bears, and was in tears after the game as he waved to the crowd.

There was split opinion this time. Some figured Favre was done because he had taken this team as far as it could go. He went out with a good season, and that's what he needed. No, no, no, said the other camp. He showed he still had it and a competitor like him won't go out when he knows he can still play.

This time he didn't leave the Packers. In April, he let the team know he would return for his 16th season.

And in 2007, Favre has added two more significant records to his seemingly endless list—most career touchdown passes and most wins by a starting quarterback.

"He looks like he's having as much fun as he always has," Harlan said. "I think he and Mike McCarthy are truly on the same page. That relationship showed up in the San Diego game this season. He throws that late touchdown pass and, when he gets to the sideline, he kind of pushes McCarthy, and Mike smiles and hugs him. That showed me something."

In 2007, Favre led the Packers to impressive wins over the New York Giants and San Diego Chargers, among others, and all despite having no running game to speak of and while working with two young receivers, Greg Jennings and James Jones.

Amazingly, the old man of the NFL was one of the game's feel-good stories of the season. And while it was nothing Favre really sought, he wasn't going to dismiss it either. Whatever worked.

After all these years, the NFL still cared about Brett Favre. ■

[opposite] Amazingly, the old man of the NFL was one of the game's feel-good stories of the 2007 season.

The Hall Awaits

In the basement of venerable Lambeau Field, a prize awaits. It's Brett Favre's No. 4 jersey, encased in glass and ready to be presented and displayed when the time is right.

It will be a special ceremony on the day Brett Favre's jersey is retired by the Green Bay Packers.

It will be a glorious fall afternoon, no doubt. Or, just maybe, it will be one of the cold, raw Lambeau days, one of those days that Favre excelled so completely in.

But the day will come, and Favre, who has never been shy about letting his emotions out, will let them all out on this special day when the Packers announce officially that no one will ever wear No. 4 for the organization again.

Really, that's just a formality since it seemed pretty clear from about 1997 that no one would ever be able to wear that number again. It would be, for lack of a better word, heresy.

Favre will then join only five other players whose number will never be worn again by the franchise: Tony Canadeo (3), Don Hutson (14), Bart Starr (15), Ray Nitschke (66), and Reggie White (92).

This is a franchise that doesn't part with its numbers, or its legacy, easily. There have been many great players, but only the best of the best of the best get a number retired. So it will be with Brett Favre some day.

Just, apparently, not yet.

Unlike the 2005 and 2006 seasons—when talk of Favre's future, or lack thereof, dominated conversation—no is really talking about whether their quarterback will retire or not. The assumption, and probably well placed, is that he'll be back in 2008.

Of course, things can change. In football they can change just like that. A severe injury, another personal crisis, a realization that the fire no longer burns, that could all alter the future. Still, the assumption now is that Favre will play for a 17th season.

And by then, he will own just about every passing record that exists—at least those he doesn't currently have.

Where to start with that?

His consecutive-games-started streak is now the stuff of myth. Since Favre started his first game for the Packers against the Pittsburgh Steelers in September 1992, 178 other quarterbacks have

(opposite) Favre's legacy is so secure that a glass-encased No. 4 jersey is sitting in Lambeau Field's basement ready to present to him when he retires.

started for every other NFL team, and 11 of them backed up Favre at one time or another.

He is an eight-time Pro Bowler. He has been named to the NFL's All-Decade Team for the 1990s. He owns the NFL records for most touchdown passes, most career completions, most career attempts, most regular season wins by a quarterback, most consecutive seasons with 20 or more touchdown passes, most seasons with 30 or more touchdown passes, most seasons leading the league in touchdown passes, most career starts by a quarterback, most consecutive 3,000-yard passing seasons, and most career interceptions.

And that's just the good stuff.

By the end of the 2007 season, he will likely own the record for career passing yardage and most career 20-touchdown seasons, both records currently owned by Dan Marino.

Not half bad for a guy who wasn't even sure he'd get a chance to play in the NFL.

But it hasn't all been perfection for Favre, and he has had his share of moments he wishes he could take back. Moments? How about years.

In a recent book written by his wife Deanna, she recounted how she had finally reached her limit with her mercurial husband. In 1999, he was drinking again and his indifference both toward her and their daughters had finally pushed Deanna to the edge. She packed his bags, left them out in front of the house, and told him to take off. He begged her to reconsider, and she did, reluctantly. And from that stage on, he has been the husband, father, and friend that she always hoped he'd be.

Maybe it was maturity or perhaps it was a fear of losing the best thing in his life, but Favre has indeed left his wild ways behind.

That doesn't mean all his relationships have ended so well. During his summer of indecision in 2006, former teammate and closer-than-close friend Mark Chmura went on a Milwaukee radio station and teed off on Favre.

"People who don't think it's all about him are fooling themselves," Chmura said on WAUK-FM in April 2006. "He's a selfish guy. He's a very selfish guy."

Favre, Chmura, and center Frank Winters made up the trio known as the "Three Amigos" in the mid-1990s. Those three were tighter than brothers, taking vacations together, playing golf, and hanging out whenever possible. Favre and Chmura even got identical tattoos on their rear ends during the high point of that relationship.

But in April 2000, Chmura was accused of sexual assault when he was found at the high school graduation party of a neighbor's daughter. In a public, sordid trial, Chmura was eventually found not guilty, but his football career was over.

What was worse, though, was that Favre never once contacted his friend to offer support or advice or even to jump on his case for being so stupid. Nothing. And to this day, Favre won't talk about it.

"You find out what people are made of, and what they are all about," Chmura said.

Favre also doesn't have a friend in former wide receiver Javon Walker. In 2004 Walker had an incredible season, catching 89 passes for 1,382 yards, scoring 12 touchdowns, and earning his first Pro Bowl berth.

Convinced he had proven his worth to the

(opposite) Favre will one day join only five other players whose number will never be worn again by another Packer player.

Packers, he demanded that his contract be renegotiated. It was a ploy that had always rubbed Favre the wrong way. Even back in 1994, when star wide receiver Sterling Sharpe planned to hold out the day before the season opener in a contract squabble, Favre verbally blasted him.

He did the same thing with Walker. But Favre, who never had a contract argument with the Packers, came from a simpler world. You sign a contract, you honor it. And when that contract is up, then you renegotiate.

Favre's public stand against Walker enraged the wide receiver who had assumed Favre would be on his side. In the end Walker blinked and

(opposite) In 2007, Favre became the NFL's all-time leader in touchdown passes. (above) Like a great general, Favre is leading his team with authority late in his career.

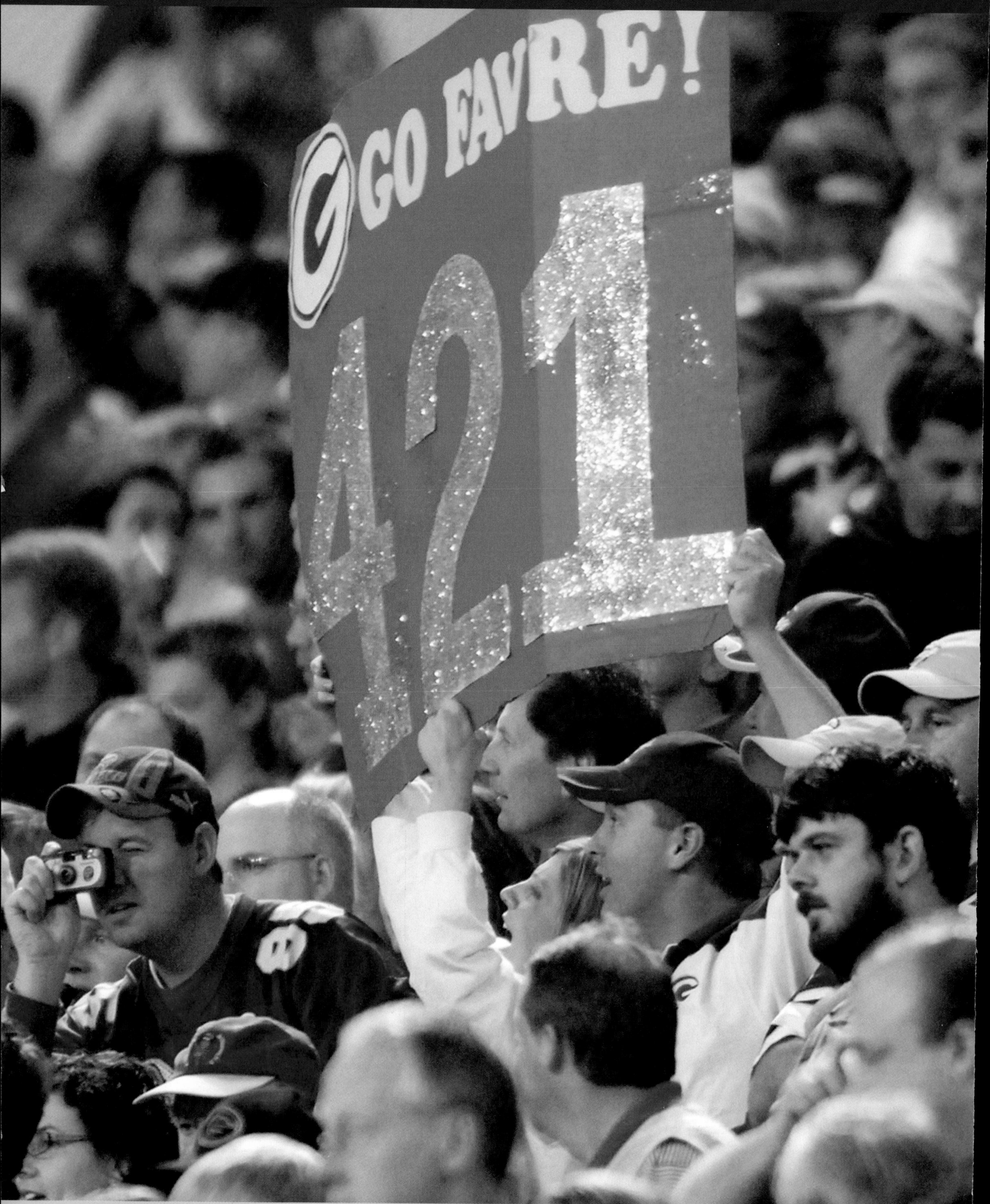
GO FAVRE!
421

reported to the Packers in 2005. But, in the first quarter of the opening game, he tore up his knee and was lost for the season. The Packers traded him the following off-season.

The criticism has bounced off Favre over the years. He has heard it all and he admits that some of it is true. Sometimes he does talk too much. Sometimes he's unfeeling and moody. He will talk for an hour to a reporter one day and brush by him the next.

He accepts that and admits, more often than not, to his mistakes. He's not perfect, but then he never claimed he was. He is who he has always been, his father's son and a guy who would still rather play football than just about anything else.

And five years after he retires, as the NFL rules state, he will be inducted into the Pro Football Hall of Fame. And what a day that will be.

And what about that day when Favre steps to the podium in front of a packed auditorium full of media to announce that he is retiring from the NFL?

Packers president Bob Harlan, for one, doesn't want to think about it.

"It will be a very sad day for this organization and for the National Football League," he said. "The last time he walks through that tunnel will be a sad day. It's like John Elway leaving Denver or Dan Marino leaving Miami."

In some ways, though, it will be worse. No one is identified more closely with the Green Bay Packers now than Brett Favre. He is the organization and everything it has stood for over the past 20 years. The Packers will move on without Favre, but it won't be easy and it won't happen quickly.

The face is older now, and the youthful eyes replaced by the tired gaze of a man who has seen everything football could throw at him. He has watched so many teammates come and go—great friends who were here one day and gone the next. In 2007 only long-snapper Rob Davis was still around from those glorious days when the Packers were not only the best team, but the best organization, in football.

And the tragedies. From his dad's death to Deanna's cancer to the death of Reggie White, the guy who was so impressed with the kid from Mississippi that he decided Green Bay was the place for him.

This much is certain. Brett Favre will leave football on his own terms. He will leave with his head up and his smile strong because he will know he played the game the way it had to be played. And that will be enough.

But Harlan, who said plans are already in place for a grand celebration when Favre does finally retire, isn't looking forward to any of it.

"I think some of it is we've taken Brett for granted," he said. "I just don't know that people understand all the special things he's done and what it's going to be like when he's not here. Those guys don't come around very often. This is a once-in-a-lifetime quarterback, and we're all going to look back and say how lucky we were to have watched him." ■

(opposite) Unlike the 2005 and 2006 seasons when talk of Favre's future dominated conversation, no one seems to be bringing up his retirement in 2007.